THESE THINGS I BELIEVE

THE WRITINGS OF WILLIAM M. GREATHOUSE

Compiled and Edited by

H. Ray Dunning and William J. Strickland

BEACON HILL PRESS

OF KANSAS CITY

CONTENTS

INTRODUCTION
WILLIAM M. GREATHOUSE AS THEOLOGIAN

AS PASTOR, professor, college and seminary president, and general superintendent, William M. (W M.) Greathouse had an all-consuming desire that the theology of the Church of the Nazarene be recognized as an expression of the classic Christian faith. It was not, he insisted, a sectarian emphasis. His earliest theological education at Bethany-Peniel College (now Southern Nazarene University), where he studied under Professor Charles McConnell, introduced him to a more balanced view of holiness teaching than prevailed in the "folk theology" of the time.

Later, at Lambuth College, a Methodist institution, Greathouse was exposed to the formative voices in Christian history. Under the tutelage of Professor J. W. Walker, he came under the lifelong influence of John Wesley. These foundational insights were broadened and deepened when, as a pastor, he continued his education at the Vanderbilt University School of Religion. He wrote his master's thesis on Wesley's doctrine of sin and perfection as interpreted by three of Wesley's major interpreters. Although urged by the Vanderbilt faculty to continue his studies toward a PhD, he had become too deeply involved in ministry by that time to do so. Learning sound methods of biblical interpretation and becoming a committed student of John Wesley's thought, Greathouse came to exercise a positive and reforming influence on the American holiness movement.

Greathouse accepted his election to general superintendent in the Church of the Nazarene with considerable reluctance. At the time, he viewed his existing post as seminary president as a calling to influence directly the theological integrity of the church. He accepted his election when he was encouraged by friends to recognize that his pulpit could become his lectern and that he could use his position and influence to shape the theological thinking of pastors and people. Throughout his tenure in office, he was recognized as a formative theological voice in the denomination.

Greathouse's holistic emphasis was often in tension with the sectarian nature of much of nineteenth-century holiness tradition. This tension subjected him to occasional criticism, sometimes of a rancorous nature. His emphasis, which profoundly shaped some of his college students, who later became professors, came to be described as "the Trevecca connection." Viewed with suspicion at first, its sound biblical character eventually came to be recognized as the enduring aspect of the holiness message by informed pastors and teachers throughout the movement.

Dr. Greathouse eventually narrowed his academic focus to two subjects—the theology of John Wesley and Paul's letter to the Romans. This concentration is obvious to anyone who reads his writing. He came to be recognized as an authority in both areas, which, as Paul Bassett once quipped, he saw as essentially the same. An analysis of Greathouse's writings, particularly on sanctification, reflects a virtual integration of these two sources, which are clearly expressions of his own theological commitments. He read widely, however, in the broad field of Christian theology, both ancient and contemporary, and gleaned insights from any source he felt was consistent with the Wesleyan perspective.

From his earliest experience in the holiness movement, Dr. Greathouse was a passionate proponent of the Wesleyan version of sanctification. He relied heavily on John Wesley's teachings and, for all practical purposes, reproduced them as his own; however, his primary theological emphasis, as these documents will validate, was on the experience of the Holy Spirit, which is the dynamic of sanctification. This emphasis transcends many of the controversial issues that have plagued holiness theologians, thus enabling him to build bridges between different perspectives. It enabled him to avoid being preoccupied with such traditional debates as crisis or process, the issue of a *second* crisis, and eradication of sin versus suppression.

While Greathouse never produced a systematic theology—his publications were largely biblical interpretations—he did seek to speak to the church through occasional essays, lectures, and articles. We have attempted to collect some of these expressions as a word to the church in the twenty-first century from a devoted and informed churchman. Because Dr. Greathouse was constantly searching for truth with a dynamic mind, it is likely that he would state some things differently today. Nonetheless, we believe that these documents can provide helpful insight in a time of crisis when the holiness movement is attempting to find its identity in an uncertain period of its history.

I
NAZARENE THEOLOGY
IN PERSPECTIVE

———⋙⋘———

The following address was given in 1969 at Dr. Greathouse's inauguration as president of Nazarene Theological Seminary. It provides an adequate summary of his understanding of the nature of Nazarene theology. It reflects his vision of how Nazarenes should view their place in the larger Christian faith. We have excerpted those pertinent passages that speak directly to this issue.

THE PREACHING of Christian perfection, with John Wesley as the chief mentor, wooed much of American Christianity during the latter part of the nineteenth century, but in the main, the Methodists were the advocates of this doctrine and experience. Increasingly, the people who espoused this doctrine, which was never meant to be a theological provincialism, found themselves unwelcome in their parent denominations. With *agapeic* hesitation but New Testament poignancy, they formed several small denominations. Three of these pilot projects formed the Church of the Nazarene in 1908—which has since that time welcomed under her wing several other denominations.

Although the denomination's founding fathers established colleges and even so-called universities, along with a few Bible schools, it was not until 1944 that the church decided to establish a graduate school of theology. My subject tonight, as I am formally installed as the seminary's fourth president, is "Nazarene Theology in Perspective."

Let me speak first of the Nazarene theological stance, and say, for one thing, about that stance that it is *catholic*. That is to say, Nazarene theology

9

stands in the classic tradition of Christian thought. The Church of the Nazarene espouses the Methodist doctrine of entire sanctification and partakes
of the Wesleyan spirit. It also adheres closely to the many important biblical and Reformation emphases, which are not distinctive to Wesleyanism.
The fifteen articles of its creed draw heavily from the twenty-five articles
of Methodism, which were, in turn, basically an abridgment of the thirty-
nine articles of the Church of England. Thus, we stand within the classical
tradition of the Christian faith.

While the Church of the Nazarene has sometimes been classified so-
ciologically as a sect-type institution that is growing into a denomination,
theologically we are not sectarian. The Nazarene *Manual* declares, "The
church of God is composed of all spiritually regenerate persons, whose
names are written in heaven." It states further,

> The Church of the Nazarene is composed of those persons who have
> voluntarily associated themselves together according to the doctrine
> and polity of said church, and who seek holy Christian fellowship, the
> conversion of sinners, the entire sanctification of believers, their up-
> building in holiness, and the simplicity and spiritual power manifest in
> the primitive New Testament church, together with the preaching of
> the gospel to every creature.

We thus believe that one is incorporated into the body of Christ by the birth
of the Spirit, signed and sealed by water baptism, and that one comes into
the Church of the Nazarene by voluntarily associating oneself with a fellowship committed to the special task of promoting New Testament holiness,
along with the worldwide preaching of the gospel.

Therefore, while Nazarenes take upon themselves the doctrine and
discipline of holiness in their endeavor to realize completeness in Christ,
they recognize that not all Christian believers are so persuaded. Positively,
they extend the right hand of Christian fellowship to all persons who are
in Christ.

Let me say further that Nazarene theology is *conservative*. "Fundamentalist" is a tag commonly attached to any Christian body that takes seriously
a particular view of the authority of Scripture. Accordingly, the Church of
the Nazarene is sometimes dubbed fundamentalist. Fundamentalism, however, is a historic phenomenon, arising in the first quarter of this century

as a protest against Protestant modernism. Today it represents the radical right of Protestantism, often allied with the radical right in politics. It espouses a view of biblical authority that we may call *biblicism*. As scientism makes a God of science, biblicism tends to make the Bible an idol.

The Nazarene position with reference to biblical authority is more Lutheran than Calvinist. For Luther, Scripture was the cradle for Christ. That is, the primary purpose of the Bible is to preach Christ. Luther's doctrine of Scripture was thus dynamic and soteriological. On the other hand, Calvin stressed the formal side of Scripture as God's written word. Although he balanced this emphasis with the idea of the *testimonium spiritus sancti internum*, Calvin's followers of the radical right have leaned toward a view of authority based on a literalist dogma concerning inspiration, which in turn has created an unnecessary theological struggle among conservatives regarding inerrancy.

Wesleyan thought has historically taken a different tack. Wesley was a preacher and an experiential theologian. In his preface to the *Standard Sermons* he wrote,

> I am a spirit come from God and returning to God: just hovering over a great Gulf; til, a few moments hence, I am no more seen; I drop into an unchangeable eternity! I want to know one thing—the way to heaven. . . . God himself has condescended to teach the way: For this very purpose, he came from heaven. He has written it down in a book. O give me that book! At any price, give me the book of God! I have it: Here is knowledge enough for me. Let me be *homo unius libri*. Here then I am, far from the busy ways of man. I sit down alone: Only God is here. In his presence I open, I read his book; for this end, to find the way to heaven.[1]

This statement is the throbbing heart of Wesley's theology of the Word; it is God's message concerning the way of salvation.

A word concerning inerrancy or infallibility is appropriate at this point, in view of the current discussion of this topic in conservative circles. During the fundamentalist-modernist controversies of the twenties, the late A. M. Hills wrote the first Nazarene theology, in which he asked, "What is the infallibility we claim for the Bible? It is infallible as regards the purpose for which it was written. It is infallible as a revelation of God's saving love in

Christ for a wicked, lost world. It infallibly guides all honest and willing and seeking souls to Christ, to holiness, and to heaven."[2]

This perspective I understand as the Lutheran-Wesleyan-Nazarene doctrine of the Word of God. It is dynamic, as opposed to idolatrous biblicism. It is indeed a conservative position, but it is not fundamentalist. The enlightened Nazarene position seems to be that of open-minded conservatism.

The heart of this conservatism is the answering conviction that our salvation is *sola scriptura* ("by Scripture alone")—that the living Word of God is the fount of all saving truth. Thus, Nazarene theology "bows to the truth of revelation."[3] The entire Nazarene theological enterprise must be carried on in obedience to God's word found in Scripture and Christ.

In addition to being catholic in spirit and conservative, Nazarene theology is *evangelical*. We stand solidly with classical Protestantism in asserting that salvation is not only *sola scriptura* but also *sola gratia, sola fide* ("by grace alone, through faith alone"). With James Arminius, we ascribe "to grace the commencement, the continuance, and the consummation of all good."[4] This grace is not only God's gracious favor toward us in Christ but also the gracious assistance of the Spirit without which we can neither turn to God to be saved nor persevere in his service. Human beings had fallen away from God as the true end of their existence and are therefore inescapably self-centered. They have neither inclination nor power of themselves to return to God; left to themselves, their only freedom is the freedom to sin. God has not, however, left his creation to itself. Through the atonement, a sufficient measure of grace is given to all persons to enable them to return to God and be saved. If death has come upon all men through the disobedience of one (the first Adam), "so by the righteousness of one [the last Adam] the free gift [of God's prevenient grace] came upon all . . . unto justification of life" (Rom. 5:18). In Wesley's words, "The grace or love of God, whence cometh our salvation, is free in all and free for all."[5]

This concept of universal prevenient grace, as opposed to irresistible grace for the elect, is a distinctly Wesleyan-Arminian contribution to theology. It seeks to preserve the scriptural paradox of divine grace and human freedom. By the free gift of God's grace, I may respond to God's proffer of salvation through Christ and find life; but, like the Pharisees, the stoners of

Stephen, I may resist the Holy Ghost and be damned. If I am saved, it is by his free grace; if I am lost, it is by my own willful perversity.

This dual emphasis is the paradox of divine sovereignty and human freedom. Only by holding these apparently contradictory truths can we ascribe to God the rightful glory for our salvation without denying the undeniable fact of our own solemn responsibility before the Almighty. When finite reason tries to resolve the tension between these two poles of revealed truth, it lands theology either in a position of absolute predestination on the one hand or of Pelagian humanism on the other. Would we not do well to leave the matter in paradox, as Scripture does?

In summary, therefore, we may say that the Nazarene stance is catholic (as opposed to sectarian), conservative (as opposed to fundamentalist), and evangelical (as opposed to Pelagian).

Second, let me speak of our distinguishing tenet, Christian perfection. It is our abiding conviction that God raised up the Church of the Nazarene for a special purpose, to bear witness to the grand truth of Christian perfection. The preamble to our Articles of Faith reads,

> In order that we may preserve our God-given heritage, the faith once delivered to the saints, especially the doctrine and experience of [entire] sanctification as a second work of grace, and also that we may cooperate effectually with other branches of the church of Jesus Christ in advancing God's kingdom among men, we, the ministers and laymen of the Church of the Nazarene . . . do hereby . . . set forth . . . the Articles of Faith, to wit . . .

Then follow our fifteen articles. That is to say, within the framework of evangelical Protestant faith, we declare that our distinguishing tenet is entire sanctification.

Our cardinal doctrine is not Christian perfection but redemption through Christ in terms of the New Testament kerygma. Within the kerygmatic proclamation, however, we lay special stress upon the fact that "for this purpose the Son of God was manifested, that he might destroy the works of the devil" (1 John 3:8). We believe that the atonement deals not simply with the fruit but also with the root of sin, not merely with the symptoms of man's moral disease but with the disease itself.

While we accent the work of full redemption, we do not do so in such a way as to place ourselves outside the mainstream of Christian tradition. Our position is not sectarian. In common with historic Christian faith, we believe that sanctification is the other side of the coin of justification, that in its broadest sense it is the total process of moral and spiritual renewal, which begins at the moment of conversion and continues to glorification. With John Wesley, however, we believe that within this process there is a second moment, a distinct and critical stage of Christian faith and life, when by the Holy Spirit God cleanses the believer's heart from the root of sin and perfects the believer in love. This critical act of God we call *entire sanctification*.

In Romans we are reminded that our Christian existence in the Spirit is an existence in the time between the times (that is, in this present time between Pentecost and the Parousia). By the grace of God we may be no longer "in the flesh, but in the Spirit, if so be that the Spirit of God dwell in" us (Rom. 8:9). But we are still in a body that is unredeemed, and we must suffer the infirmities of the flesh—the radical effects of sin in our bodies and minds, the scars from past sinful living, our prejudices that hinder God's purposes, our neuroses that bring emotional depressions and cause us at times to act out of character, our temperamental idiosyncrasies, our human weariness and fretfulness, and a thousand faults our mortal flesh is heir to. As St. Paul reminds, "We have this treasure in earthen vessels, that the excellency of the power may be of God, and not of us" (2 Cor. 4:7).

A full-orbed doctrine of Christian perfection must place the truth of holiness within the framework of this present age, which is characterized by these infirmities of the flesh. Thus, Paul declares that we have been saved by hope—the hope of that final stroke of sovereign grace that shall bring to consummation that grand work of sanctification that began when we were converted. This complete transformation is the hope of the resurrection. Wesley would agree with the late Karl Barth, who comments on this Romans passage: "If Christianity be not altogether restless eschatology, there remains in it no relationship whatever to Christ."[6] Thus, Wesleyanism is in perfect accord with "the theology of hope."[7]

I realize that many people scorn such a doctrine of imperfect perfection. To deny, however, the possibility of being filled with the Spirit and knowing God's perfect love because we are still finite creatures subject to the limitations of earthly existence, is to miss something that is vital to New Testament Christianity. We therefore subscribe to the Wesleyan paradox of Christian perfection. The full truth is not gained by removing the tension between the two poles (perfect / not yet perfect) but by holding these two truths with equal emphasis. Only thus does the Christian life flower into Christlikeness.

We devoutly believe that God has entrusted to the Church of the Nazarene the grand depositum of this New Testament teaching of heart holiness. If we cease to groan after this perfection in Christ, if we fail to make this emphasis the focus of salvation truth in our preaching, if we do not pay the full price for Pentecost in our individual experience and in the life of the church, we will forfeit our Nazarene birthright and our very reason to exist. Most tragic of all, we will fail God, who commissioned us to spread scriptural holiness over these lands.

II

JOHN WESLEY'S THEOLOGY OF CHRISTIAN PERFECTION

This address was given in 1988 to the Wesley Fellowship in Bristol, England. It reflects both Dr. Greathouse's knowledge of the Wesley corpus and his dependence on the eighteenth-century leader for his understanding of Christian perfection. It is obvious Dr. Greathouse finds little, if anything, in Wesley's explanations with which to disagree. The themes emphasized in this address remained continuing aspects of his teaching and preaching throughout his career. Parts of this address appear verbatim in several places in his writing.

THE APPEARANCE in 1935 of George Croft Cell's *The Rediscovery of John Wesley* signaled a reappraisal of the English reformer as a first-rank theologian. This watershed study claims that in Wesley's gospel, "The special interests in and tremendous emphasis of early Protestantism upon the doctrine of justification by faith . . . was reunited, as in the New Testament, with the special interest of Catholic thought and piety in the ideal of holiness or evangelical perfection."[1]

Cell argues convincingly that "homesickness for holiness" constitutes "the internal kernel of Christianity." The essence of this holiness is Christlikeness, "no more, no less," such as caught the imagination of St. Francis of Assisi.[2] This "lost accent of Christianity" fell into the background of interest in early Protestantism. Cell quotes Adolf Harnack's observation that Lutheranism in its purely religious understanding of the gospel went to such an extreme in its reaction against Roman Catholicism that it neglected too much the moral problem—the "be holy, for I am holy." "Right here," Cell continues, "Wesley rises to mountain heights. He restored the neglected doctrine of holiness to its merited position in the Protestant understanding of Christianity."[3]

In 1790, the year before his death, Wesley wrote, "This doctrine is the grand depositum which God had lodged with the people called Methodists; and for the sake of propagating this chiefly he appeared to have raised us up."[4] In *Understanding the Methodist Church*, Nolan B. Harmon comments, "The doctrine of Christian perfection has been the one specific contribution which Methodism has made to the church universal."[5] Although he acknowledges that this doctrine has sometimes been an embarrassment to Methodism, Colin Williams writes,

> It is only in the context of the total expression of the Christian life represented in Wesley's theology that his doctrine of perfection can be understood, for perfection is simply the climax of the limitless faith in God's grace that shines through every part of his theology. It is here that his theology comes to a focus.[6]

The Meaning of Perfection

Wesley always defined perfection as the fulfillment of the Great Commandment: "The loving the Lord our God with all our heart, mind, soul, and strength; and the loving our neighbor, every man, as our own souls."[7] Such fulfillment "implies that no wrong temper, none contrary to love, remains in the soul; and that all the thoughts, words, and actions, are governed by pure love."[8] In "The Scripture Way of Salvation," he says, "It is love excluding sin; love filling the heart, taking up the whole capacity of the soul. . . . How strongly [does this] imply being saved from all sin! For as long as love takes up the whole heart, what room is there for sin therein?"[9]

It is the thesis of this brief monograph that Wesley's understanding of perfection is best defined teleologically. For him, the perfect Christian is not one who is flawless or infallible but one who is "conformed to the end" of his existence (i.e., to love God supremely and his fellow man as his own soul). "The attitude that ultimately determines his theology," Harold Lindstrom observes, is that

> everything is directed toward the perfection of man as the condition of his glorification. A natural consequence . . . is that salvation becomes

a process of sanctification by which man is increasingly purified and perfected to attain his final end. And since love was for Wesley the very essence of sanctification, it too must be teleologically determined in the same way: Love must be accommodated to the progress towards the goal of salvation. It is also the highest value in the scale. Church, ordinances, outward acts, and inward tempers, all else acquire value only insofar as it leads to love, the highest goal of human zeal.[10]

The Greek *teleios*, generally rendered "perfect" in the Authorized Version, has a rich and varied meaning and needs at least an introductory survey in order to assess Wesley's doctrine of perfection. Kittel sees the term as most characteristically meaning "totality." The person "who does the 'whole' will of God" is perfect, whose "heart is 'undivided' in obedience to God." This statement encapsulates both the Old Testament and New Testament ideas of perfection.[11]

Etymologically, *telos* has a variegated meaning. In reference to sacrifices, it means "whole, without blemish," then complete in compass, with nothing left out. A thing is perfect that has been brought to or arrived at the *telos*—therefore, that which is actualized. Biologically, it suggests full grown, mature, or adult.[12]

In their commentary on Aristotle's *Metaphysics*, Antonio Royo and Jordan Aumann point out that St. Thomas Aquinas sees three different ways of using the term: "When a thing lacks nothing due to its nature; where there is neither excess nor defect as regards its powers of operation; and when it has attained its proper goal or end."[13]

Quotations might be multiplied to show that, for Wesley, perfection has all the above shades of meaning. It is heart purity, or singleness of intention. It is blamelessness before God, wholeness or completeness of devotion to him. The perfect Christian is mature as in an adult son or father in faith. But it appears that these and related ideas are best subsumed under the more inclusive concept of perfection as fulfilling the one end of glorifying God in all we do and thereby realizing our true raison d'être.

It is an axiom of Christian faith that the glory of God is the absolute end of our existence. This truism presupposes no transcendental egoism in God, as some impious philosophers have dared to say; for God is not *eros* but *agape*: overflowing love and goodness seeking to communicate itself to his creatures. Paraphrasing St. Thomas, Royo and Aumann write, "He does not work because of any need, as if seeking something that he lacks, but only out of goodness, to communicate to creatures his own overflowing happiness."[14] The glory of God is the end and purpose of all creation. Even the incarnation of the Word and the redemption of the human race have no other finality than the glory of God: "And when all things are made subject to him, then the Son himself will also be subject to him who subjected all things to him, that God may be all in all" (1 Cor. 15:28).[15]

St. Paul exhorted the Corinthians: "Whether therefore ye eat, or drink, or whatsoever ye do, do all to the glory of God" (1 Cor. 10:31). Wesley comments, "In all things, whatsoever, whether of a religious or civil nature, in all the common as well as sacred, actions of life, keep the glory of God in view, and steadily pursue in all this one end of your being, the planting or advancing the vital knowledge and love of God, first in your own soul, then in all mankind."[16]

Royo and Aumann add, "After the glory of God, and perfectly subordinated to it, the Christian life has for its end or goal the sanctification of one's own soul."[17] In common with Scripture and classical Christian thought, Wesley sees two ends in the process of our sanctification by the Spirit: the final end and the relative or proximate end. He expresses these two ideas succinctly in his note on Philippians 3:12 ff.: "There is a difference between one that is perfect and one that is *perfected*. The one is fitted for the race (verse 15); the other, fitted for the prize."[18] The final end of Christian experience is the beatific vision when we shall be glorified with Christ;[19] the relative or proximate end, to be "fitted for purpose," conformed to the divine end of our existence, as spelled out in the Great Commandment.

When Wesley insists on the possibility of perfection in this life, he always means *evangelical* perfection, the relative or proximate perfection commanded by the law and promised in the gospel.

In *A Plain Account of Christian Perfection,* Wesley insists, "The whole law under which we now are is fulfilled by love (Romans 13:9, 10). Faith working or animated by love is all that God now requires of man."[20] Again, he asks, "How is 'love the end of the commandment?' (1 Timothy 1:5)."[21] His answer: "It is the end of every commandment of God. It is the point aimed at by the whole and every part of the Christian institution. The foundation is faith, purifying the heart; the end love, preserving a good conscience."[22] He concludes,

> It is well you should be thoroughly sensible of this—"the heaven of heavens is love." There is nothing higher in religion; there is, in effect, nothing else; if you look for anything but more love, you are looking wide of the mark, you are getting out of the royal way. And when you are asking others, "Have you received this or that blessing?" if you mean anything but more love, you mean wrong; you are leading them out of the way, and putting them upon a false scent. Settle it in your heart, that from the moment God has saved you from all sin, you are to aim at nothing more, but more of that love described in the thirteenth of [First] Corinthians. You can go no higher than this, till you are carried into Abraham's bosom.[23]

What Is Sin?

Now if obedience to the Great Commandment is the end of the Christian life, sin is the missing of *that* mark—not loving God and neighbor. The problem of sin, however, is not that we are poor marksmen; rather, we miss the mark because we choose to aim at the wrong one: we have turned from God our true end to self the false end. Wesley explains the reason for this distortion:

> The unrenewed will of man is wholly perverse, in reference to the end of man. Man is a merely dependent being; having no existence or goodness originally from himself; but all he has is from God, as the first cause and spring of all perfection, natural and moral. . . . And thus man was created looking directly to God, as his last end; but, falling into sin, he fell off from God, and turned into himself. Now, this infers [sic] a total apostasy and universal corruption in man; for where the last end is changed, there can be no real goodness. And this is the case of all men in their natural state: They seek not God but themselves. Hence though many fair shreds of morality are among them, yet "there is none that doeth good, no, not one." For though some of them "run well," they are still off the way; they never aim at the right mark. Whithersoever they move, they cannot move beyond the circle of self. They seek themselves,

they act for themselves; their natural, civil, and religious actions, from whatever spring they come, do all run into, and meet in, this dead sea.[24]

Prevenient Grace

This pessimistic view of fallen human nature must, however, be balanced by Wesley's doctrine of prevenient grace:

> For allowing that all the souls of men are dead in sin by *nature*, this excuses none, seeing there is no man that is in a state of mere nature; there is no man, unless he has quenched the Spirit, that is wholly void of the grace of God. No man living is entirely destitute of what is vulgarly called *natural conscience*. But this is not natural: it is more properly termed *preventing grace*. Every man has a greater or less measure of this, which waiteth not for the call of man.[25]

Fallen humanity thus is not left in the "Dead Sea" of egocentricity. Through his prevenient grace, God seeks to "turn" each individual, first awakening, convicting, and calling that one back to himself; then, as a person responds, enabling that one to repent and trust Christ for salvation. In this divine-human process a person is "converted," turned back to God as the true end of that one's existence.

Conversion becomes an accomplished fact in justification. Pardoned from sin and restored to the favor of God through Christ, the believing soul is renewed by the Holy Spirit in the love of God. Wesley asserts,

> At the same time that we are justified, yea, in that very moment, sanctification begins. In that instant we are born of God, born from above, born of the Spirit: there is a *real* as well as a *relative* change. We are inwardly renewed by the power of God. We feel "the love of God shed abroad in our heart by the Holy Ghost which is given unto us"; producing love to all mankind, and more especially to the children of God; expelling the love of the world, the love of pleasure, of ease, of honour, of money, together with pride, anger, self-will, and every other evil temper; in a word, changing the earthly, sensual, devilish mind, into "the mind which was in Christ Jesus."[26]

It is, however, not long before "sin revives" in our hearts, and we become painfully aware of "two principles" in ourselves.[27] While the *reign* of sin is broken and we enjoy the witness of the spirit that we are children of God, we discover the *remains* of sinful corruption in our hearts, "a propensity to pride, self-will, anger, revenge, love of the world, yea, of all evil, . . . such a depth of corruption, as without the clear light of God, we cannot possibly conceive."[28]

Despite this inner cleavage of the mind and heart, "from the time of our being born again, the gradual work of sanctification takes place" if we avail ourselves of the proffered grace of God. Wesley explains,

> We are enabled "by the Spirit" to mortify the deeds of the body, of our evil nature; and as we are more and more dead to sin, we are more and more alive to God. . . . It is thus that we wait for entire sanctification; for a full salvation from all our sins—from pride, self-will, anger, unbelief; or, as the Apostle expresses it, "go on to perfection." But what is perfection? The word has various senses: here it means perfect love. It is love excluding sin; love filling up the heart, taking up the whole capacity of the soul.[29]

It is instructive here to heed the words of Gordon Rupp:

> Wesley kept firmly to the two doctrines of original sin and of total depravity. . . . [He] accepted the doctrine of total depravity, though his doctrine of prevenient grace, and of the objective results of the atonement took some of the sting out of it. But, positively, this doctrine affirms two important truths concerning the Christian view of history. First, what has gone wrong is no merely negative thing, an appalling series of accidents. . . . It is, as the Bible insists, no mere deprivation, deprivation of God, but it is a depravation, a depravity, positive rebellion, mutiny, hostility to God, a restless egotism, a perseverance of idolatry by which man ever and again under manifest disguises puts himself on the altar and worships the creature. And, second, this is an all-in-all affair. . . . No race, culture, century can contract out of this solidarity of judgment. . . .[30]

But the depth of this tragedy must be attached with the heights of grace; the solidarity of mankind in Adam viewed against the solidarity of mankind in the Second Adam, Jesus Christ, of whom Charles Wesley sings, "Head of all mankind art Thou." Total depravity is set in the context of total grace, of the great salvation.

To which Colin Williams appropriately responds, "At a time when our theology has recaptured the depth dimension of sin and has learned again and again the true 'pessimism of nature' that marks this awareness, it is more imperative that we know the heights of the 'optimism of grace' that flow from the faith relationship with Christ, the Victor over sin and death."[31]

John Wesley's contribution to the church universal is precisely this "optimism of grace," which he found promised in Scripture, and verified by hundreds of living witnesses.

The Role of the Holy Spirit

Implicit in all that Wesley taught about perfection was the conviction that from first to last it is the work of the sanctifying Spirit. "The title 'holy' applied to the Spirit of God," he said, "does not only imply that he is holy in his own nature, but that he makes us so; that he is the great fountain of holiness to his church; the Spirit from whence flows all the grace and virtue, by which the stains of guilt are cleansed, and we are renewed in all holy dispositions, and again bear the image of the Creator."[32]

If pure love of God and man is the essence of Christian perfection, the sanctifying Spirit is its agency. Wesley asserts, "Entire sanctification is neither more nor less than pure love; love expelling sin, and governing both the heart and life of the child of God. *The refiner's fire purges out all that is contrary to love.*"[33]

Although Wesley recognized that certain Old Testament saints anticipated by faith the New Testament promise of heart purity, he saw clearly that perfection as a common privilege for "God's people was the distinctive promise of the Messianic Age of the Spirit."[34]

John N. Oswalt has pointed out that two prophecies were of special significance for Wesley: Joel 2:28-29 and Ezekiel 36:25-27. The coming of the Spirit promised in Joel refers to the inauguration of the Christian faith: the gift of the Spirit for all who believe in Christ. Ezekiel 36:25-27, however, promises heart cleansing by the deeper working of the Holy Spirit within the being of one already a believer.[35]

In his *Explanatory Notes upon the Old Testament*, Wesley applies the Ezekiel passage expressly to the New Testament promise of heart holiness. The expression "sprinkle" in verse 25 "signifies both the blood of Christ sprinkled upon the conscience to take away their guilt . . . and the grace of the Spirit sprinkle[d] in the whole soul, to purify it from all corrupt inclinations and dispositions." The "new heart" promised in verse 26 is "a new frame of soul, a mind changed, from sinful to holy, from carnal to spiritual; a heart in which the law of God is written (Jer. 31:33); a sanctified heart, in which the almighty grace of God is victorious, and turns it from all sin to God." The "spirit" promised in verse 27 is "the Holy Spirit of God, which is given to, and dwelleth in all true believers," which causes them to keep God's judgments "sweetly, powerfully, yet without compulsion; for our spirits, framed by God's Spirit to a disposition suitable to his holiness, readily concurs."[36]

Holiness as Love

"John Wesley's conviction," says Paul Bassett, is "that there is an experience of grace subsequent to regeneration, instantaneously receivable, which renders the believer capable of acting and being in complete conformity to the Great Commandment,"[37] that is, of "loving the Lord our God with all our heart, soul, mind, and strength; and . . . our neighbor, every man, as ourselves, as our own souls."[38] This, says Wesley, is "the end of every commandment of God . . . the point aimed at by the whole and every part of the Christian institution. The foundation is faith, purifying the heart; the end love . . ."[39]

The teleological structure of Wesley's theology is here clearly seen in the way everything is directed to the final end, with all else regarded as means to this end. "The object of salvation," says Lindstrom "is the restoration in man of the love of God. This is effected by faith. Faith is only the means, the end is love."[40]

Wesley's doctrine may be defined as a theology of holy love. Mildred Wynkoop says, "The principle by which to understand Wesley's doctrine is love to God and man, in the biblical sense of the word. Love is the dynamic of theology and experience. Love, structured by holiness, links all we know of man. Love is the end of the law. It is the goal of every step in grace and the norm of the Christian life in this world."[41]

Lindstrom writes in the same vein: "The essence of perfection and the goal of faith [is] . . . love. Seen in this way, therefore, the Christian life is development in love. Perfection comes to mean perfection in love."[42] From the moment we are justified until we are glorified, there is but "[one] *kind* of holiness; . . . only in various *degrees*, in believers who are distinguished by St. John into 'little children, young men, and fathers.' The difference between the one and the other properly lies in the degree of love."[43]

Before the purification of the believer's heart in entire sanctification, that person's love is mixed with fear and sinful self-love. But when this deeper work of heart cleansing has occurred, that person's whole soul is now consistent with itself. That one now bears the one *undivided* fruit of the Spirit, and experiences *pure* love of God and man. That individual now enjoys perfect love—love excluding sin; love filling his heart, taking up the whole capacity of his soul.

Sanctification as Single-Mindedness

The teleological character of Wesley's doctrine is [further] seen in his unswerving insistence that Christian or evangelical perfection is not a matter of "sinlessness" but of such "singleness."

In his sermon "On the Single Eye," Wesley asserts, "What the eye is to the body, the intention is to the soul. . . . 'If thine eye be single,' singly fixed on God, 'thy whole body,' that is, all thy soul shall be filled with holiness and happiness."[44] "The recovery of the image of God . . . is the one thing needful on earth. . . . For to this end man was created."[45] To Mrs. Bennis, he wrote, "A will steadily and uniformly devoted to God is essential to sanctification, but not an [*sic*] uniformity of joy or peace or happy communion with God."[46] "Purity of heart is to will one thing" (Kierkegaard).

But even though the glory of God is the aim of all entirely sanctified Christians, they still miss that mark because of their human weaknesses. "This much is certain," Wesley writes to a Miss March,

> They that love God with all their heart and all men as themselves are scripturally perfect. And surely such there are; otherwise, the promise of God would be a mockery of human weakness. Hold this fact. But then remember, on the other hand, you have this treasure in an earthen vessel; you dwell in a poor, shattered house of clay, which presses down the immortal spirit. Hence all your thoughts, words, and actions are so imperfect, so far from coming up to the standard (that law of love which, but for the corruptible body, your soul would answer in all instances), that you may well say till you go to him you love: every moment, Lord, I need the merit of Thy death.[47]

In a more theological vein he writes,

A perfection such as enables a person to fulfill the whole law, and so needs not the merits of Christ—I acknowledge no such perfection; I do now and always did protest against it. "But is there no sin in those who are perfect in love?" I believe not. But be that as it may, they feel none; no temper contrary to pure love, while they pray and give thanks continually. And whether sin is suspended or extinguished, I will not dispute. It is enough they feel nothing but love.[48]

He claims further he never talked with a person who denied "that a truly sanctified person does involuntarily fall short in divers instances of the rule marked out in the thirteenth chapter of [First] Corinthians. And that on this account, they continually need their Advocate with the Father."[49]

In his *Plain Account*, Wesley gives a theological formulation of his views: The best of men still need Christ in his priestly office, to atone for their omissions, their short-comings (as some not improperly speak), their mistakes in judgment and practice, and their defects of various kinds. For these are all deviations of the perfect law, and consequently need an atonement. Yet that they are not properly sins, we apprehend may appear from the words of St. Paul, "He that loveth, hath fulfilled the law; for love is the fulfilling of the law" (Rom. 13:10). . . . I believe there is no such perfection in this life as excludes these involuntary transgressions which I apprehend to be naturally consequent on the ignorance and mistakes inseparable from mortality. Therefore *sinless perfection* is a phrase I never use, lest I should seem to contradict myself. I believe, a person filled with love is still liable to these transgressions.[50]

Consequently, "even perfect holiness is acceptable to God only through Jesus Christ."[51]

This "imperfect perfection" clearly calls for a distinction between two kinds of sin: voluntary and involuntary. Wesley states, "In terms of sin in the absolute sense, as measured by the 'perfect law' there is no such perfection in believers." It is in terms of the sin of conscious violation of the law of love that a believer can enjoy perfection, "a perfection of unbroken conscious dependence on Christ."[52]

Wesley's first definition of sin is most clearly defined in another letter to Mrs. Bennis: "Every voluntary breach of the law of love is sin; and nothing else is."[53] This breach is "sin properly so called." C. Ryder Smith supports such a position as being the primary meaning of *harmartia*, "the one compendious word for sin" in the New Testament. "As in the LXX [Septuagint, Greek translation of the OT]," Smith observes, "'to sin' still means to 'aim at a wrong mark and so to miss the right one.' Again as in the LXX, 'sin' is always *against God*. Where this is not explicit, it is implicit. To 'sin against a brother' is to sin against God even as man's love of his 'neighbour' is an outcome of his love of God."[54]

But as we have already seen, even those who enjoy "pure love to God and man" and in singleness of heart are "so far perfect as not to commit sin" in the proper sense of *harmartia*, still "sin," that is, "miss the mark" of flawless obedience to God's perfect law of love. This dialectical tension between gospel and law is essential to the Wesleyan doctrine lest it lead to pharisaical pride. Colin Williams judiciously observes, "We need to hold in a constant, dialectical relationship the offer of freedom from the sin of separation in our personal relationship with Christ and the continuing sin in the lives of the 'perfect' when judged by the perfect law. By the very gift of the unbroken moment-by-moment relation to Christ, the believer should become increasingly aware of the need for continuing transformation of his total existence."[55]

The tension is seen in Paul as that between the "now" and the "not yet" of our redemption in Christ. "For all have sinned, and are fallen short of God's glory" (Rom. 3:23, Wesley's translation). That "glory" is the *imago Dei* lost in the fall and now being progressively restored in a process of sanctification by which human beings are increasingly purified and perfected to attain their final goalcomplete conformity to the image of God's Son (Rom. 8:29). St. Paul writes, "And we all, with unveiled face, beholding the glory of the Lord, are being changed into his likeness from one degree of glory to another; for this comes from the Lord who is the Spirit" (2 Cor. 3:18, RSV).

Two passages of significance for this view of "imperfect perfection" are Philippians 3:10-15 and Romans 8:10-29. Though by the grace of God in Christ we may have been brought to spiritual maturity (love made perfect), we are still but "Christians in the making" (E. Stanley Jones). We have not yet attained the mark of final Christlikeness for which we were claimed of God through the gospel; but we do have a singleness of purpose, which permits the Spirit to carry us forward toward that goal with steadiness. As P. T. Forsyth expresses that idea, sounding quite Wesleyan, "Our perfection, therefore, is not to be flawless, but to be in tune with our redeemed destiny in Christ."[56] This quality is the thought of Philippians 3:12-14.

In Romans, we are reminded that our Christian existence is an existence in the "time between the times," that is, in "the present time" between Pentecost and the Parousia. By the grace of God we may no longer be "in the flesh, but in the Spirit, if so be the Spirit of God dwell in" us (Rom. 8:9). But we are still in a body that is unredeemed and must suffer "the infirmities of the flesh"—the racial effects of sin in our bodies and minds, the scars from past sinful living, our prejudices that hinder God's purposes, our neuroses that bring emotional depressions and cause us at times to "act out of character," our temperamental idiosyncrasies, our human weaknesses and failures, and a thousand faults to which our mortal flesh is heir. St. Paul reminds us, "But we have this treasure in earthen vessels, that the excellency of the power may be of God, and not of us" (2 Cor. 4:7).

A full-orbed doctrine of Christian perfection must locate holiness within the framework of "this present age" characterized by these "infirmities of the flesh." Thus Paul declares that we have been "saved in . . . hope" (Rom. 8:24, NKJV)—the hope of that final stroke of sovereign grace that will bring to glorious consummation that grand work of sanctification that began when we were converted. This final perfection is the hope of the Resurrection. Wesley would surely agree with Karl Barth, who comments on this passage, "If Christianity be not altogether restless eschatology, there remains in it no relationship whatever to Christ."[57]

True, there are those who scorn such a doctrine of "imperfect perfection." But to deny the possibility of being perfected in love by the infilling of the Holy Spirit because we are still finite creatures subject to human limitations and failures is to miss something vital to New Testament Christianity. We therefore subscribe to "the Wesleyan paradox" of Christian perfection. The full truth is not gained by removing the tension between the two poles ("perfect"—"not yet perfected") but by holding these two truths with equal emphasis. Only thus does the Christian life flower into Christlikeness.

"Beloved, we are God's children now; it does not yet appear what we shall be, but we know that when he appears we shall be like him, for we shall see him as he is. And every one who thus hopes in him purifies himself as he is pure" (1 John 3:2-3, RSV).

III

ON ENTIRE SANCTIFICATION

This paper was delivered at the First Theology Workshop, sponsored by the Council of Education and the Department of Education of the Church of the Nazarene in July of 1958. Dr. Greathouse was then dean of religion at Trevecca Nazarene College. It reflects his awareness of issues that were beginning to emerge regarding the church's tradition concerning entire sanctification, issues that later flowered in what many have acknowledged to be an identity crisis. It furthermore reflects an enduring characteristic of his ministry, the interaction between academic inquiry and personal experience. His own experience was the constant throughout his entire career, even though his inquiring mind went through a growing process. At the age of thirty-nine, his theological honesty, insight, and catholic perspective were already in evidence. In this early presentation, he is wrestling with the creed of the church and relying heavily on secondary sources. As his understanding matures—as we shall see—he eventually comes to focus more on the teaching of Scripture and John Wesley. We have omitted some sections of this paper that were lengthy reports of secondary interpretations.

IT IS OUR abiding conviction that God raised up the Church of the Nazarene for a special mission—to bear witness to the precious experience of entire sanctification. It is our raison d'être to assure men that "the blood of Jesus Christ . . . cleanseth us from all sin" (1 John 1:7). Apart from this peculiar emphasis, we have no reason to exist as a denomination.

Our central doctrine, however, is not entire sanctification but redemption through Jesus Christ. In summarizing his gospel to the Corinthians Paul writes, "For I delivered to you as of first importance what I also received, that Christ died for our sins in accordance with the scriptures, that he was buried, that he was raised on the third day in accordance with the scriptures" (1 Cor. 15:3-4, RSV). The gospel is the proclamation of the redemptive activity of God in Jesus Christ. This message is the New Testament kerygma, and it is central and fundamental. Within this message however, we lay special stress upon the fact that "for this purpose was the Son of God manifested, that he might destroy the works of the devil" (1 John 3:8). We insist upon the total adequacy of that redemption. We declare that the atonement deals not simply with the fruit but also with the root of sin, not merely with the symptoms of humans' moral disease but with the disease itself. Paul Sherer accuses Barth, Brunner, and Niebuhr[1] of perverting the Pauline dictum in Romans 5:20 to read, "But where grace abounded, sin did much more abound." However, with St. Paul, we believe that "where sin abounded, grace did much more abound."

While we accent the work of entire sanctification, we do not do so in such a manner as to place ourselves outside the main stream of Christian tradition. Our position is not sectarian. In common with historic Protestantism, we believe that sanctification in its broadest and most comprehensive sense is a process of moral and spiritual renewal beginning with regeneration and continuing to glorification. Most of us would perhaps agree that the term is used sometimes in an objective sense to affirm the separation, which marks the true people of God: "But you are a chosen race, a royal priesthood, a holy nation, God's own people" (1 Pet. 2:9, RSV). We, however, are convinced that "sanctification" has a narrower and more specific meaning in the Scriptures. Within the process of the believer's renewal in the image of God, there is a distinct critical moment when that one is baptized with the Holy Spirit and cleansed from the root and inbeing of sin. This critical act of God we call "entire sanctification."

✳ ✳ ✳

This act frees from sin and brings the believer into a condition of perfect love. Human consecration precedes the crisis of cleansing; divine consecration ensues, "a state of entire devotement to God." The passage from the one to the other is, from the human standpoint, faith; from the divine standpoint, the baptism with the Holy Spirit. The ground of all this transformation is the atoning work of Christ. The most precious experiential aspect of entire sanctification is undoubtedly "the abiding indwelling presence of the Holy Spirit." Living within the temple of our hearts, he is himself the witness to God's purifying grace in our lives. [We] recognize that there are different phases of this gracious experience. To one, it appears superlatively as heart purity. To another, conscious of the fullness of the Spirit, it is the baptism with the Holy Spirit or the fullness of the blessing. Yet another with Wesley is impressed that the experience is preeminently a participation in God's agape love; he speaks of perfect love or Christian perfection. Others prefer to call it simply Christian holiness. These various names represent facets of this glorious grace of full salvation.

It is virtually impossible to say anything new on this distinguishing tenet of our movement. In a tentative way, I should like simply to suggest what I consider some of the crucial issues we must face in thinking through this grand depositum of our church—this first. Then I shall enumerate some of the biblical and theological resources I have discovered that have strengthened my own understanding of this grand work of God in the soul.

First, critical areas that must continue to challenge our best study and thought are the following:

1. Do the scriptures teach a second epoch in Christian experience that actually effects a cleansing from original sin? How can we answer [W. E.] Sangster's contention that no man can know the depths of his own heart? What must we say to Niebuhr's teaching of the inevitability of sin even in the life of grace?[2]

2. What is the nature of perfect love? Is perfect love compatible with the mind's tendency to rationalization? With our own personal shortcomings? With our insensitivity to social issues? What shall we say relative to our remaining humanity—the self and its instincts?

3. How is entire sanctification related to the atonement? Is the atonement a propitiation only, or is it actually a destruction of sin?

4. Are we correct in identifying entire sanctification with the Spirit baptism? Are we giving proper emphasis to the person and work of the Holy Spirit in our teaching and preaching of entire sanctification?

5. Would we do well not to de-emphasize the second crisis, but to lay heavier stress on the lifelong process of sanctification, the gradual work of God in our souls by which we are renewed in the image of God?[3]

Obviously, this brief paper cannot adequately come to grips with these issues. This week, I understand, we shall take time to grapple earnestly and scripturally with these and other questions. Recognizing the limitations of my own knowledge and experience, I hesitate even to suggest lines of approach. I can at least intimate the direction my own mind has taken. In so doing I will also suggest the biblical and theological resources I have discovered to be of help to my own thought.

Before I embark on this task, permit me a word of personal testimony. Lest I leave the impression that there are doubts as to the validity of this great work of God, I will share with you my own discovery of the fullness of the Spirit. During my entire ministry, I have sought to follow peace with all men and the sanctification without which no man shall see the Lord. Coming from a nominal Methodist background, I was from the beginning impressed with the crucial significance of our distinguishing doctrine. To the best of my ability, I seriously grappled with the implications of this teaching. I sought to appropriate the grace and preach it specifically. As I look back, I can trace various stages of development in my Christian experience, but I recall in particular the painful awakening that came to me as a result of the faithful witness of some students who had found a relationship with God that was foreign to me. At first, I resented their testimony and argued against it. I dubbed it mysticism. I defended my own spiritual mediocrity and rationalized obvious deviations from the inner law of the Spirit of life in Christ Jesus. Gradually, however, a hunger began to gnaw at my heart.

Then came the day when I admitted to myself that I had never entered into the rest of faith. While reading the fourteenth chapter of John's Gospel, a faith was suddenly given me. In a moment utterly unique, the Comforter came to indwell my heart. At this instant, a work of God was wrought in my soul fully as supernatural, fully as transforming, as that evening several years previous when instantly I recognized his presence and began quietly to affirm, "He has come! The Comforter has come!" at a Nazarene home mission campaign I became a new creature in Christ Jesus.

Since that day when the Holy Spirit came to indwell the temple of my heart, I have known a new intimacy in my relationship with God. At times, the emotional tide has ebbed away, but from that hour, my life has moved on a permanently deeper level. Before then I had operated more under my own power than the power of the Spirit; since then God has enabled me to live in the comfort of the indwelling Spirit. About many things, I may be uncertain; of one thing, I am sure—the Holy Spirit has come to my life in his abiding, sanctifying fullness. Out of this newfound certainty flowed a new power in my preaching and teaching. As far as I am concerned, my credentials to teach this precious doctrine are primarily my personal knowledge and experience of the indwelling Holy Ghost.

Now, to consider one or two critical issue we face in formulating this doctrine:

1. Do the Scriptures teach full salvation? Does the second crisis effect a radical cleansing from sin? Does entire sanctification deal a death blow to original sin, or depravity? *Here indeed is the Achilles' heel of our position* (emphasis added).

After critically examining the texts upon which Wesley built his doctrine of entire sanctification, Sangster concludes,

Has he made out his case? Is the doctrine well within the Scriptures? Has modern scholarship materially affected the problem, or is the exegetical question the same in substance as it was in the eighteenth century? Did he find the doctrine in the Bible, or carry preconceived ideas to it? . . .

Our enquiry is, as yet, too incomplete to give a categorical answer to all those questions. But this can be said with confidence. The passing of two centuries and all the solid biblical scholarship, which has been crowded into them, have not in themselves rendered Wesley's position untenable. In short, grammar, and the closest textual scrutiny undertaken in its light, have not determined the issue either way. *The theological presuppositions which subtly affect exegesis have more to do with decisions on this matter than the biblical student might care to concede.* As we have surveyed Wesley's textual foundations, we have noticed the shadows of dubiety cast by scholarship on a translation, or interpretation, here and there, but, for the most part, the stones stand.[4]

If we take the New Testament at face value, we dare not place any limits on the grace of God. The difficulty arises when we seek to interpret this cleansing in terms of personal experience. It would seem to this writer that the critical question relates to *the nature of sin*. Permit me to make this observation: *To preserve our message we must continue to make Wesley's distinction between objective and subjective sin.* We cannot begin from Calvinistic premises (or neo-Calvinistic premises) and affirm the possibility of Christian perfection. While we would do well to heed the Calvinists' warning against Pharisaism, we would be wise to stay with Mr. Wesley in his contention that sin *in the proper sense* always involves a compliance of the will. John L. Peters quotes Wesley:

> Nothing is sin, strictly speaking, but a voluntary transgression of a known law of God. Therefore, every voluntary breach of the law of love is sin; and nothing else, if we speak properly. To strain the matter farther is only to make way for Calvinism. There may be ten thousand wandering thoughts and forgetful intervals without any breach of love, though not without transgressing the Adamic law. But Calvinists would fain confound these together.[5]

It is in the *subjective* sense alone that the Christian is "freed from sin." Peters asks, "Had [Wesley] forgotten how easily the mind can be clouded by its own rationalizations, how loath and incompetent for honest self-appraisal man is, and how insensitive to social issues and to their own shortcomings the most saintly have often been? Perhaps he had. Confronted with such considerations, however," Peters answers, "Wesley would probably have maintained that, even so, his definition was relevant. Any sin which involved guilt, he would reiterate, required intelligent freedom of choice. Where the highest possibility had been presented and choice had been made of anything else, therein was sin, 'properly so called.'"[6]

In Niebuhr's sense, of course, no Christian can expect to love perfectly. We are involved in a moral situation of compromised good; however, Niebuhr's impossible "higher possibility" is Wesley's impossible "full conformity to the perfect law." Wesley admitted an *objective* standard from which the most saintly "inevitably" fall short. Accordingly, Wesley had an objective definition of sin: "*All* deviation from perfect holiness *is sin,*" he wrote. Since even those subjectively perfect in love may still fall short of this objective standard of righteousness, he refrained from speaking *in this context* of "sinless perfection." Right here is the area of apparent contradiction, but it is primarily a matter of terminology. From the subjective standpoint, perfect love is a defensible concept; from the objective standpoint, it is not, because, in Wesley's words, "there is no man living who does not fall short of the law of love."

To make this distinction does not mean that we must be blind to what Calvin and Niebuhr are trying to get us to see. We Wesleyans have not always been truly Wesleyan. We have been guilty of neglecting this objective phase of Wesley's teaching. In the contemporary scene, Niebuhr and others have stabbed us awake to the truth of objective sin. We need not, however, forfeit our message under this barrage of criticism. An interesting sidelight to this issue is the recent confession of Niebuhr to some of his colleagues that his greatest theological mistake has been his strong criticism of Wesley's doctrine of Christian perfection. . . . Let us continue, therefore, to make Wesley's distinction between subjective and objective sin. Niebuhr would have us "confound these together." The outcome can be only hopeless confusion.

But what shall we say concerning our remaining humanity—the self and its instincts? Clearly, this problem is a subjective one. I must confess that Dr. Sangster's searching criticism in *The Path to Perfection* has given me pause, particularly chapter 17, titled "Is It Self-Deception, Sanctification, or Peace?" The questions he raises are well worth our careful consideration. I do not, however, believe we must concede his main point, that, since no man can know the depths of his own heart, we dare not witness to the experience of heart holiness.

✳ ✳ ✳

This fact a genuinely sanctified man knows—that by the power of the indwelling Holy Ghost his life has been lifted to the level of the spirit. As St. Paul reminds us, "But ye are not in the flesh, but in the Spirit, if so be that the Spirit of God dwell in you" (Rom. 8:9). Therefore, with St. Paul he can testify, "For the law of the Spirit of life in Christ Jesus hath made me free from the law of sin and death" (v. 2). With trembling heart he can witness: "I am crucified with Christ: nevertheless I live; yet not I, but Christ liveth in me: and the life which I now live in the flesh I live by the faith of the Son of God, who loved me, and gave himself or me" (Gal. 2:20).

In conclusion, I wish to state in summary style several buttresses to our position:

First, a new view of the atonement. Contemporary theology is coming more and more to appreciate the dramatic motif of the atonement, which in the early centuries of Christian thought crystallized into the ransom theory. P. T. Forsyth, and more recently Gustaf Aulen, has exerted considerable influence in effecting this shift of appreciation. For many years it was the fashion to pass by the first eleven hundred years of Christian history as barren with regard to atonement doctrine. The church, it was held, subscribed to a fantastic, grotesque view of Christ's death. Not until Anselm developed his satisfaction theory, it was argued, did the church come to a reasoned doctrine of the atonement.

Many theologians have repented of this error; that is, they are beginning to think again. They are coming to see that behind the crude ransom theory, as it came to be expressed, is a true scriptural view of Christ's atoning work, *a dramatic motif.* Christ's incarnation, crucifixion, resurrection, exaltation, and his gift of the Spirit are acts in a single drama. The atonement is a divine movement, both objective and subjective, both finished and continuing. New Testament exegetes have gone back to the documents of our faith and found them filled with this view. The idea of propitiation is there also, but Christ's death is more than propitiation, it is redemption—the destruction of sin: "For this purpose the Son of God was manifested, that he might destroy the works of the devil" (1 John 3:8). Not only does the atonement provide for man's justification, but it is also the fountain for his sanctification. Justification deals with the symptoms of man's disease; sanctification heals man at the center of his being. The atonement is the ground of it all. It is this classical motif of *Christus Victor,* which forms the background of the great sanctification passages of the New Testament, Romans 6 through 8 in particular: "Knowing this, that our old man has been crucified with him, that the body of sin might be destroyed, that henceforth we should not serve sin" (6:6).

Observe how the incarnation, crucifixion, resurrection, and the gift of the Spirit are synthesized in these verses:

There is therefore now no condemnation to them which are in Christ Jesus . . . For the law of the Spirit of life in Christ Jesus hath made me free from the law of sin and death. For what the law could not do, in that it was weak through the flesh, GOD sending his own Son in the likeness of sinful flesh, and for sin, CONDEMNED SIN IN THE FLESH: that the righteousness of the law might be fulfilled in us, who walk not after the flesh, but after the Spirit. (Rom. 8:1-4, emphasis added)

The incarnate Son of God has met sin on its own ground, that is, in human personality, and utterly routed the foe on the very battlefield where it had entrenched itself. Through Christ, GOD has pronounced the doom of sin in the flesh—he has completely sanctified human nature. This sanctification is mediated to us through our faith-union with Christ.

Present soteriological though is providing a framework for our doctrine of sanctification. In an organic view of New Testament soteriology, entire sanctification is an integral part, the subjective counterpart of Christ's objective history. Here is solid ground upon which we may stand.

Second, a new appreciation of the work of the Holy Spirit. A few years ago, Nels Ferrè wrote,

Modern Christianity has been rude and faithless in its limiting of the Holy Spirit. It has lived by things visible, by man's experience or history, rather than by things invisible and divine. We have come close to killing the nerve both of individual improvement and of historic effort by our faithless stress on our sin. That is not our message. The message is that sin need neither "reign" nor "remain." . . . How much we need the stress of the New Testament on the victory of the Holy Spirit if we let him. There is no limit to what he can do. The only limit is our acceptance of him.[7]

There are heartening signs that this situation may be beginning to change. Strangely enough, it is within the field of eschatology that the emphasis is beginning to shift. Biblical theology is coming to recognize that the New Testament is thoroughgoingly eschatological. Everything is oriented to the end, the Parousia.

In a very real sense, however, the future is here. In Jesus Christ the kingdom of God has broken into history. The kingdom was present germinally in Christ. It came upon his generation as he, by the Spirit of God, cast out demons. It was established in power, however, by his death, resurrection, and enthronement at the right hand of God. Its consummation awaits his second coming in glory. Between these two events, his first and second advents, stretches *the messianic age of the Spirit.*

Commenting on Acts 1:3, F. F. Bruce writes,

> At Christ's first coming the age to come invaded the present age; at His second coming the age to come will have altogether superseded the present age. Between the two comings the two ages overlap; Christians live temporally in the present age while spiritually they belong to the heavenly kingdom and enjoy the life of the age to come.[8]

The gift of the Spirit *is* the life of the age to come, the pledge and foretaste of the inheritance that shall be ours at the Parousia. The outpoured Holy Spirit is the Promise of the Father, the hallmark of this dispensation. Dr. George Hendry's recent work, *The Holy Spirit in Christian Theology*, devotes an entire chapter to this theme. He writes,

> The incidence of the Spirit is interpreted in the New Testament as the fulfillment of Old Testament prophecy, which had given a place of central importance to the Spirit in the eschatological hope of Israel. In the latter days of Israel's history, when the visitation of the Spirit had ceased to be known as a present reality in the life of the people and had become an object of future hope, this hope received a definite shape in the prophecy of an outpouring of the Spirit, which would be permanent and universal.[9]

Here again we see the solid biblical ground upon which is based our teaching of entire sanctification through the baptism with the Holy Spirit.

Finally, the new understanding of agape, love. This final point I need not labor. [Anders] Nygren's monumental work *Agape and Eros*, while not winning universal agreement in every detail, has revolutionized the concept of Christian love. . . . Agape is God's own love, which is given to us by the Holy Spirit. In Sangster's words, agape is "love—in love's divinest feature." And here we must put our greatest stress.

Of absolute or sinless perfection, we must not speak. There is offered to the hungering and thirsting Christian, nevertheless, a perfect love, upon the condition of self-surrender and simple trust, as a bounty of the Spirit: "Thou shalt love the Lord thy God with all thy heart . . . and thy neighbor as thyself" (Luke 10:27). The heart may here and now, by the Spirit, be perfected in this love.

Through the gift of the Spirit the *intellect* may be exalted to a supreme love of God—the love of imaginative appreciation. The imagination of the perfected heart is no longer stirred by the thoughts of sin but is fired by the vistas of divine truth. Through the gift of the Spirit, the *emotions* may be exalted to a supreme love of God—the love of affection. In such a heart, the expulsive power of a higher affection has cleansed the inner stream of the desires so that the soul rejoiced in God alone and that which is in accord with his holy will. And through that same Spirit the *will* is exalted to a supreme love of God—the love of devotion. Every antagonism to the will of God is purged away in the refining fire of the divine Spirit of love. Though the mind must be occupied with the mundane interests of this temporal existence and though the soul be devoid of holy ecstasy in the ebb and flow of human emotion, yet in the heart perfected in love there is always one constant factor—the devotion of the will. "We love him none the less during this period," says Fénelon, "than in those in which we make him the most tender protestations. True love rests in the depths of the heart."

Perfect love is therefore the perfection that God offers upon the simple condition of responsive faith. It is the knitting of the heart into a holy unity about God and manifests itself in the Christlike love of neighbor. It is the agape of God shed abroad in the heart: the love of goodwill, which refuses to limit itself to those who will reciprocate it and which reveals its chief glory in returning good for evil and in going the second mile. Perfect love is the Sermon on the Mount become practicable. It is the thirteenth chapter of First Corinthians incarnate in human personality by the power of the indwelling Holy Spirit. It is personal, ethical, social love, redemptive, and sacrificial.

Perfect love, however, is not static. It is never realized in its fullness here below. Nevertheless, in self-crucifixion and faith, in receptivity and response, this love is mediated by the Holy Spirit and realized within as a dynamic of victorious living: "Be ye therefore perfect, even as your heavenly Father . . . is perfect" (Matt. 5:48).

IV
WHO IS THE HOLY SPIRIT?

‎

This article was originally published in the Herald of Holiness, *May 10, 1972. Later that year during the denomination's General Assembly, "tongues-speaking" had become an issue in the church, and Dr. Greathouse was being maligned by some for being "soft on tongues." That misrepresentation of his beliefs clearly resulted in his not being elected general superintendent at that assembly. This failure was rectified in 1976. This essay both puts that accusation to rest and further reflects his emphasis on the authentic Wesleyan teaching of the work of the Holy Spirit as being in the mainstream of Christian thought as well as soundly biblical. We have omitted a section of the essay that was simply a survey of several theories of the Spirit-filled life. The substance of his argument is found here.*

SOME OF US have seen a kaleidoscope, a box of colored glass fragments, which yields an ever-changing pattern of symmetrical beauty when viewed through the triangular tube of mirrors, which multiplies and coordinates their "broken lights."

The Bible doctrine of the Spirit is kaleidoscopic. In the Book we see an ever-changing pattern of beauty with respect to the Spirit, from the opening lines of Genesis where he is brooding over the chaos to the closing chapter of Revelation where "the Spirit and the bride say, come" (22:17).

The New Testament, however, sums up the doctrine in one phrase: "the Spirit of Christ." To John the Baptist, God said, "Upon whom thou shalt see the Spirit descending, and remaining on him, the same is he which baptizeth with the Holy Ghost" (John 1:33). As the promised Messiah, Jesus was the *Bearer* and *Baptizer* with the Holy Spirit.

41

At his baptism, Jesus was revealed as the Bearer of the Spirit. The descending dove marked him as the anointed of God. Pentecost disclosed Jesus as the Spirit-Baptizer.

In these twin events, the Spirit of God became the Holy Spirit of our Lord Jesus Christ, never to be separated from him. Jesus the Christ became the supreme manifestation of the Holy Spirit, as that Spirit became the Medium through whom Christ comes to indwell and sanctify his church.

• *Christ is the Pattern of the Spirit-filled life.* His entire life—from the moment of his miraculous conception to that climactic moment when he offered himself by "the eternal Spirit" (Heb. 9:14) as our perfect Sin Offering—was a manifestation of the Holy Spirit.

The Holy Spirit is therefore the *Christ*-spirit. "The fruits [*sic*] of the spirit are the virtues of Christ," in Schleiermacher's fine phrase. God gave the Spirit "without measure" to Jesus (John 3:34, NASB), so that he becomes the norm of the Spirit-filled human life.

It was not until Jesus gave up his life forgivingly on the cross that that pattern was complete: "Christ also suffered for us, leaving us an example, that ye should follow his steps. . . who, when he was reviled, reviled not again; when he suffered, he threatened not; but committed himself to him that judgeth righteously" (1 Pet. 2:21, 23).

As H. Wheeler Robinson says, the Spirit of Jesus is "the Spirit of the Cross." The only kind of spirituality the New Testament recognizes is that which makes us Christlike in our suffering, forgiveness, compassion, and caring.

• *Christ's glorification is the absolute condition of the gift of the Spirit.* At the Feast of Tabernacles, Jesus announced, "The man who believes in me . . . will have rivers of living water flowing from his inmost heart" (John 7:38, Phillips). John immediately comments, "But this spake he of the Spirit, which they that believe on him should receive: for the Holy Ghost was not yet given; because that Jesus was not yet glorified" (v. 39).

The Spirit was active through the ancient dispensation. Yet the New Testament says unequivocally that the *Holy* Spirit was not given until Christ was "glorified"—that is, not until after the crucifixion, resurrection, and ascension.

Peter makes this point clear in his Pentecostal sermon: "This Jesus hath God raised up, whereof we all are witnesses. Therefore being by the right hand of God exalted, and having received of the Father the promise of the Holy Ghost, he hath shed forth this, which ye now see and hear" (Acts 2:32-33).

• *What does this new relationship mean with respect to the Christian's experience of the Spirit?*

First, the Pentecostal baptism with the Spirit is a gift specifically for the Christian dispensation. The Spirit is that "better thing" reserved for New Testament saints (Heb. 11:40). It was this baptism of which the Ephesian disciples had not heard (Acts 19:2). Dwight L. Moody confessed, "For the first seven years of my Christian life I was as ignorant of the Holy Spirit as the disciples at Ephesus." What about you?

Second, this Pentecostal gift means that Christ himself is personally present in our hearts by the indwelling Spirit.

Concerning the promised Paraclete, Jesus said, "I will come to you" (John 14:18). Earlier in this chapter, he had promised his literal coming at the end (vv. 1-3); here he speaks of his spiritual return in the Spirit (see vv. 22-23). Again he prayed, "Sanctify them . . . that the love wherewith thou hast loved me may be in them, *and I in them*" (17:17, 26, emphasis added). So Paul can equate "the Spirit of God" with "the Spirit of Christ" in the experience of the believer and then referred to him as "Christ . . . in you" (Rom. 8:8, 10).

The Christian experience of the Holy Spirit means, primarily, to have "Christ . . . formed" in us (Gal. 4:19). The very Christ who was formed in the womb of the Virgin Mary by the Holy Spirit is formed in our hearts by the selfsame Spirit! In the new birth, Christ constitutes himself our very Life, so that we can say, "For to me to live is Christ" (Phil. 1:21).

The full meaning, however, goes far beyond conversion. Paul prays for God's saints who are now the "habitation of God through the Spirit . . . that Christ may *dwell* in [their] hearts by faith" (Eph. 2:22; 3:17, emphasis added). The Greek verb is quite specific. It means "to take permanent residence [as against transitory]." Thus, the *Good News Translation* (GNT) renders, "that Christ may make his home in your hearts." That is, that he may become the Host who makes your heart his holy dwelling place, so that he sanctifies every nook and cranny of your being.

This experience is the same as being "filled with all the fulness of God" (3:19), since *in Christ* "dwelleth all the fulness of the Godhead" (Col. 2:9). All of this meaning is in Paul's thought when he later urges these Christians: "be filled with the Spirit" (Eph. 5:18).

Who is the Holy Spirit? He is the Spirit of Christ. He is self-effacing. He does not speak of himself, but of Christ. His work is to reveal Christ *in* us and *through* us.

Any concept of spirituality that promises some advance beyond Christ-likeness through the indwelling Spirit is spurious.

Paul's version of Pentecost is found in Romans: "God's *love* has been poured into our hearts through the Holy Spirit which has been given to us" (Rom. 5:5, RSV, emphasis added). His word here (agape), says F. R. Barry, "describes what human life begins to look like when the Spirit gets to work on it."

Jesus himself was the perfect incarnation of agape (God's kind of love). When the Spirit sanctifies and indwells us, the fruit of his working is Christ-like agape. This implication is why Paul says, "Now if any man have not the Spirit of Christ, he is none of his" (Rom. 8:9). This test is a supernatural one—our lives are the gift and work of Christ's Spirit. It is also an ethical test—"for we realise that our life in this world is actually his life lived in us" (1 John 4:17, Phillips).

The Wesleyan Answer

Who is the Holy Spirit? The New Testament is clear. On the pages of the Christian book, the Holy Spirit is always and everywhere the Spirit of Jesus Christ. By his glorification "the last Adam became a life-giving spirit" (1 Cor. 15:45, RSV). Paul can even say, "Now the Lord *is* that Spirit" (2 Cor. 3:17, emphasis added). In the Holy Spirit, the resurrected one manifests his resurrection power.

"Just as we have borne the image of the earthy," Paul writes, so "we shall also bear the image of the heavenly" (1 Cor. 15:49, NASB). Christ will finally change our lowly existence to be like his glorious heavenly existence, "by the exertion of the power that He has even to subject all things to Himself" (Phil. 3:21, NASB).

We are predestined to be conformed to the image of the Son, "that he might be the firstborn among many brethren" (Rom. 8:29). And so "we all, with un-

veiled face, beholding as in a mirror the glory of the Lord, are being transformed into the same image from glory to glory, just as from the Lord, the
Spirit" (2 Cor. 3:18, NASB). The Holy Spirit is the sanctifying Spirit of Christ.

It was the spiritual genius of John Wesley that he saw with penetrating
clarity that this sanctifying ministry of the Spirit lays at the very heart of
Christ's redemptive activity.

In his classic interpretation of John Wesley, George Croft Cell says,

Wesley's theocentric doctrine of Christian experience is first, last, always a doctrine of the Holy Spirit. Holiness is the primary attribute of
the Christian church. Holiness is the essential quality of Christian experience. Holiness is the third term of the Trinitarian revelation of God.
This is the highest conceivable position for the doctrine of holiness in
the Christian faith and interpretation. One of Wesley's earliest Oxford
sermons notes that "the title holy applied to the Spirit of God does not
only denote that he is holy in his own nature, but that he makes us so;
that he is the great fountain of holiness to his Church. The Holy Spirit
is the principle of the conversion and entire sanctification of our lives."[1]

Cell then observes that "Wesleyan theology was preeminently a doctrine of the Holy Spirit. The experiential witness of a spirit of holiness as
the necessary companion of Christian faith may even be called a special interest of Wesleyanism. It has in this respect a certain individuality of tone.
But this is no afterthought or separate thought of the Christian revelation;
it is of the essence of it."[2]

The doctrine of sanctification is therefore no "theological provincialism" of Wesleyanism. It is rather our witness to the grand New Testament
truth that the Spirit of Christ is the *sanctifying* Spirit and that all his minis-
trations are to the end of making us holy and Christlike persons.

The finest New Testament scholarship supports the correctness of this
high Wesleyan estimate of the Holy Spirit as the hallowing Spirit of Christ.
Just as Christ redeemed us through his blood, he also transforms us into his
own image by the Holy Spirit. This transformation is what the New Testament is all about, and it is what Wesleyanism has always tried say.

45

The Error of Corinthianism

We are now in a position to evaluate another view of the Spirit's work that misses the central biblical teaching.

In the Corinthian church, Paul was face to face with some who seemed to believe that the Spirit's ministry effected a level of spirituality that elevates one to a point *beyond* "mere" Christlikeness and holiness. According to a recent, able study, the Corinthians of this party "maintained that glossolalia is the main (or only) evidence of possession by the Spirit . . . Only those Christians who have this gift are classified as spiritual."

In dealing with this teaching that true spirituality moves the believer beyond the Lord into a realm of mysticism and ecstasy, Paul reminds these persons that before they were Christians they had these very same kinds of experiences they were now making the hallmark of the *Holy* Spirit of Christian experience.

"You know how," he writes, "in the days when you were still pagan, you would be seized by some power which drove you to these dumb heathen gods" (1 Cor. 12:2, NEB margin). "There is no doubt at all," Shrenk comments, "that Paul intends to say here, 'the truly spiritual is not marked by a being swept away; that is precisely the characteristic of your previous fanatical religion.'"

Paul then continues, "For this reason I must impress upon you that no one who says 'A curse on Jesus!' can be speaking under the influence of the Spirit of God. And no one can say 'Jesus is Lord!' except under the influence of the Holy Spirit" (v. 3, NEB).

When you were still heathen religionists, Paul is saying, the essence of your worship was this feeling of being "carried away" by some spirit; now, however, you experience the *Holy* Spirit and you experience him supremely when he leads you to submit yourselves absolutely to Jesus Christ and confess him as sovereign Lord of life—in intelligible speech and ethical behavior.

Some scholars think these Corinthians were actually cursing Jesus in the ecstasy of their tongues-speaking. More likely, from their supposed position of exalted spirituality, they were saying, "Anathema Jesus," in contempt of "mere" Christianity, which places supreme emphasis upon the incarnation and the experience of "Jesus Christ, and him crucified" (2:2).

All this simplistic stuff was too elementary for these super-religionists! It was too tame and unexciting for these persons who must have visions and revelations and ecstasies.

St. Paul, however, refused to acknowledge such a view as representing the *Holy Spirit*. Rather, the apostle goes on to show with great tact, skill, and gentleness that the real proof that we are spiritual is that we have been cleansed from such spiritual egotism and transformed into the image of him who said, "I am among you as he that serveth" (Luke 22:27).

The gifts of the Spirit are not "spiritual" things (*pneumatikon*; 1 Cor. 12:1) for personal aggrandizement or individual spiritual superiority. They are rather grace gifts (*charismata*; vv. 4-11), which make us loving and humble like Jesus. They are gracious endowments that enable us to contribute to "the common good" of the undivided body of Christ. It may even be questioned whether a gift can be said to "exist" for the individual if it is not employed for the sake of building up the body of Christ in loving unity.

Then Paul comes to the lofty pinnacle of New Testament truth when he pens, "And now I will show you the best way of all" (v. 31, NEB), without which any and all gifts are absolute *zero*—the way of agape love. To understand 1 Corinthians 13, we must see it in this setting, which shows that Christlike love is *the gift* of the Spirit.

With characteristic genius, John Wesley makes Paul's point clear:

Another ground of . . . a thousand mistakes is, not considering deeply, that love is the highest gift of God; humble, gentle, patient love; that all visions, revelations, manifestations whatever, are little things compared to love; and that all the gifts are either the same with, or infinitely inferior to, it.

It were well you should be thoroughly sensible of this—the heaven of heavens is love. There is nothing higher in religion; there is, in effect, nothing else; if you look for anything but more love, you are looking wide of the mark, you are getting out of the royal way.

And when you are asking others, "Have you received this or that blessing?" if you mean anything but more love, you mean wrong; you are leading them out of the way, and putting them upon a false scent. Settle it in your heart, that from the moment God has saved you from all sin, you are to aim at nothing more, but more of that love described in the thirteenth chapter of [First] Corinthians. You can go no higher than this, till you have reached Abraham's bosom.[3]

V
THE BAPTISM WITH
THE HOLY SPIRIT

———∞∞∞———

In the 1970s, a controversy erupted in the Wesleyan Theological Society, triggered by a paper delivered by Herbert McGonigle, demonstrating the difference between John Wesley and the modern holiness movement on the meaning of Pentecost. The latter had followed the teaching of John Fletcher rather than Wesley in identifying entire sanctification with the baptism with the Holy Spirit. This controversy soon spread to the churches, threatening to disrupt the unity of the people. Dr. Greathouse, with his usual irenic temperament, engaged the task of attempting to bridge the divide between the two interpretations by good exegesis. This paper is an expression of this mediating position. The perceptive reader will notice that he did not actually address the point at issue between the two positions, namely whether or not Pentecost was a "second work of grace" in the lives of the apostles. His exegetical conclusions leave the option open for either interpretation but clearly implies the pristine Wesleyan high view of the initiating Christian experience of the new birth.

"BAPTIZED WITH [or in] the Holy Spirit" (and the equivalents) is a phrase practically limited to the Gospels and Acts (Matt. 3:11; Mark 1:8; Luke 3:16; John 1:33; Acts 1:5; 11:16). The Epistles speak of believers being indwelt by the Holy Spirit (Rom. 8:9, 11; 1 Cor. 3:16; 6:19; 2 Cor. 6:16; Gal. 4:6; Eph. 2:22; 5:18; 1 Thess. 4:8; 2 Tim. 1:14; Titus 3:5; cf. John 14:15-16, 23; 1 John 3:24; 4:12, 15) or filled with the Spirit (Eph. 5:18; cf. 3:19); they contain only one reference to Spirit baptism (1 Cor. 12:13), which most interpreters view as a reference to the action of the Spirit by which believers are incorporated into the body of Christ.

49

John Wesley's pneumatological terminology follows this New Testament pattern. For him "all true believers to the end of the world"[1] are baptized with the Spirit—that is, have received the gift of the Spirit, which came at Pentecost. This Spirit is the *Holy* Spirit, "the principle of our conversion and entire sanctification to God." Wesley explains,

> The title "holy," applied to the Spirit of God, not only indicates that he is holy in his own nature, but that he makes us so; that he is the great fountain of holiness to his Church; the Spirit from whence flows all the grace and virtue, by which the stains of guilt are cleansed, and we are renewed in all holy dispositions, and again bear the image of our Creator.[2]

Wesley's doctrine of salvation is "post-Pentecostal." For him the Christian era did not properly begin until the day of Pentecost when the exalted Jesus bestowed upon the waiting company of believers the promised gift of the Holy Spirit. His theology is not based upon the Luke-Acts passages, which recount the transition of persons from the old to the gospel dispensation, but upon the apostolic doctrines of God, Christ, and the Spirit delineated in the Epistles.

In his first standard sermon, Wesley gives his classic definition of Christian faith:

> Christian faith is . . . not only an assent to the whole gospel of Christ, but also a full reliance on the blood of Christ; a trust in the merits of his life, death, and resurrection; a recumbency upon him as our atonement and our life, *as given for us*; and *living in us*; and, in consequence hereof, a closing with him, and cleaving to him, as our "wisdom, righteousness, sanctification, and redemption," or, in one word, our salvation.[3]

By this precise definition, *only persons after Pentecost could have proper Christian faith.* We see therefore why Wesley said the disciples were not "converted" until Pentecost. Their relationship to Christ was not perfected until that day, when the glorified Jesus bestowed the Holy Spirit to apply the sanctifying benefits of his death and enthrone him as the living Christ within their hearts. In the *Notes*, Wesley states unequivocally that the disciples were justified during the time of Jesus' earthly sojourn with them. Commenting on John 15:3 ("now ye are clean"), he says, "All of you to whom I now speak are purged from the guilt and power of sin."[4] Although Wesley is silent on the subject of entire sanctification of the 120 on the day of Pentecost, his note on

John 14:23 should not be overlooked. Jesus' promise here, Wesley observes, "implies such a large manifestation of the divine presence and love, that the former, *in justification*, is nothing in comparison of it."[5]

It is well known that it was John Fletcher, Wesley's admired friend and designated successor, who found in the Spirit baptism language of Acts more specific reference to the sanctifying fullness of the Spirit. Wesley was tolerant of Fletcher's position, but he objected to its theological implications because he was convinced the New Testament teaches that all believers have received the Holy Spirit.[6] For his part, Fletcher argued that to denominate all believers truly *baptized* with the Spirit permitted the church—if it did not encourage it to do so—to live beneath its spiritual privileges in this dispensation of the Holy Ghost. Wesley and Fletcher never resolved their difference of viewpoint (which, as we hope to point out, reflects a proper New Testament tension).

The standard Methodist theologians all followed Wesley's lead; but Fletcher's view survived, and in America, at least to some degree, flourished through the broad distribution of his *Last Check* and the widely circulated *Memoirs* and *Letters* of Hester Ann Rogers.[7]

It was Charles G. Finney, a New School Calvinist, who actually became the catalyst for the fusion of the doctrines of Christian perfection and the baptism with the Holy Spirit in American Methodist thought. Finney had come to this view during his Oberlin College lectures in 1838 and 1839, in which he announced his discovery of the links between covenant and promise in the Old Testament, and Jesus' covenant and promise in the New Testament of his continuing presence through the Comforter. As Timothy Smith shows, the content of the sanctification promised in the covenant and provided by the Spirit is personal holiness and social righteousness.[8]

George O. Peck, editor of the Methodist *Christian Advocate*, read Finney's lectures as they appeared in *The Oberlin Evangelist*, and in the fall of 1840 Peck himself began to equate entire sanctification and the Spirit's baptism. The idea was immediately picked up by Methodist preachers and writers, and by 1855 reports of Methodist camp meetings and revivals referred to persons being "baptized" or "filled with the Spirit," and used these expressions interchangeably with the older Wesleyan terms for holiness. In 1856 Phoebe Palmer embraced this position (after considerable struggle), and her next major book was titled *Promise of the Father for the Last Days*. This teaching soon became the standard one of the holiness movement.[9]

Finney's finally developed theological position, however, remains in question. Neither his systematic theology nor his more popular *Views on Sanctification* equate the baptism of the Holy Ghost with heart holiness. In addition, when he addressed the Oberlin Council on Congregationalism in 1871 on "The Baptism of the Holy Ghost," his stress was not upon sanctification but the "enduement of power" received in the baptism.[10] This idea of the Spirit's empowerment became the prevailing emphasis of Moody and Torrey and indeed of the entire school of thought associated with the Keswick and Northfield conventions. According to this Calvinistic understanding, the baptism with the Holy Spirit provides an infilling that only counteracts the sin nature while energizing the believer for holy life and witness.

About the turn of the [twentieth] century, modern Pentecostalism emerged from the attempted fusion of Wesleyan and Pentecostal ideas. The Pentecostal Holiness Church separated the baptism of the Holy Ghost (evidenced by speaking in tongues) from the purification of entire sanctification, making the baptism a "third work of grace." Other Pentecostals, notably the Assemblies of God, have consistently denied the realizability of entire sanctification by faith. For them sanctification is a lifelong process completed only at death, with the empowering baptism being understood as an ecstatic experience. This view seems to be, in general, the understanding of most branches of neo-Pentecostalism. In this teaching the *gifts* rather than the *fruit* of the Spirit provide evidence one has "had his baptism."

Among Wesleyans, the present discussion of the subject of Spirit baptism is the outcome of several factors:

1. A renewed interest in biblical theology with its attendant insistence upon honest, careful exegesis and the final authority of Scripture over all theological tradition. This emphasis has created a climate and methodology that has made the inquiry almost inevitable.

2. The 1973 paper read by Herbert McGonigle to the Wesleyan Theological Society on "Pneumatological Nomenclature in Early Methodism."[11] This paper sparked the series of studies by the Wesleyan Theological Society.

3. The reemergence on a broad scale of the Pentecostal doctrine of Spirit baptism, along with the claim that this teaching derives logically from Wesleyanism.[12] Many Wesleyan scholars object vigorously to this facile linkage of Pentecostalism and Wesleyanism. These persons are concerned to preserve the New Testament teaching that the Spirit came not to exalt himself and his gifts but Christ. They see a danger of a Corinthian pneumatology supplanting the Johannine and Pauline teaching that the only true evidence of the Spirit's sanctifying fullness is holiness of heart and Christlikeness of life. For these, the debate is more than an academic exercise about the meaning of a certain phrase; the discussion rather touches on the very heart of the Wesleyan message.

In this essay, the writer is "thinking aloud" in an endeavor to find for himself a synthesis that will be scripturally sound and experientially valid. It is his thesis that the traditional view of Christian experience reflects an almost entirely individualistic valuation of the gift of the Spirit, to the neglect of the New Testament teaching of the church as the *community* of the Spirit. We must be willing to permit the Scriptures to speak for themselves and set our proper Wesleyan emphasis upon entire sanctification as the Spirit's distinctive work within the context of the communal significance of Pentecost. Some theological groundwork is therefore necessary. A failure to give attention to this wider background, this writer believes, accounts for the present polarity that marks the so-called Spirit baptism debate.

The Significance of Pentecost

Pentecost marked the full inauguration of Jesus as the Christ. In his sermon on that epochal day, the apostle Peter declared, "Let all the house of Israel know assuredly, that God hath made that same Jesus, whom ye crucified, both Lord and Christ" (Acts 2:36). At his baptism Jesus had been *identified* as Messiah; by his resurrection and enthronement he was *installed* as Messiah. As the glorified Christ, he was "designated Son of God in power" (Rom. 1:4, RSV; cf. Acts 13:33) and "became a life-giving spirit" (1 Cor. 15:45, RSV; cf. 2 Cor. 3:17-18). At his baptism he was revealed as the *Bearer* of the Spirit; on the day of Pentecost he became the *Baptizer* with the Spirit (John 1:33; Acts 2:32-33).

From the New Testament perspective, Christ's baptism with the Holy Spirit was of twofold significance: (1) It created the church as his Spirit-filled body, the eschatological community of salvation; (2) it fully inaugurated the new covenant, with the pledge of personal inward sanctification for all believers.

1. The Formation of the Church as the Body of Christ

Dr. H. Orton Wiley puts this truth in graphic language:

The Holy Spirit formed the Church at Pentecost. . . . As the natural body is possessed of a common life which binds its members together in a common organism; so the Holy Spirit sets the members of His spiritual body as it pleases Him, united them into a single organism under Christ as its living Head. God did not create men as a string of isolated souls, but as an interrelated race of mutually dependent individuals; so also the purpose of Christ is not alone the salvation of the individual, but the building up of a spiritual organism of interrelated and redeemed persons. . . .

The Holy Spirit is therefore not only the bond that unites the individual soul to Christ in a vital and holy relationship; but He is the common bond that unites the members of the body to each other, and all to their living Head. The Spirit is the life of the body, and since His inauguration at Pentecost, has His "See" or seat within the Church. . . . Previous to Pentecost, the mild showers of the Holy Spirit descended upon Israel in drops of saving grace; but in such manner as each gathered for himself. This continued until the Incarnation, when Christ gathered into Himself the full stream of the Holy Spirit; and when these channels of faith were completed and every obstacle removed, the Holy Spirit on the day of Pentecost came rushing through the connecting channels into the heart of every believer. Formerly there was isolation, every man for himself; now it is an organic union of all the members under their one Head. This is the difference between the days before and after Pentecost.[13]

2. The Enactment of the New Covenant

Pentecost, furthermore, marked the new dispensation of the Holy Spirit. The prophets of the old economy promised an eschatological gift of the Spirit, which would be permanent and universal. The endowment would be given first to the Messiah-Servant (Isa. 11:1-2; 42:1-4), then to the entire people of God (Isa. 32:14-17; 44:3; Joel 2:28-29), not only removing their guilt but also sanctifying their natures (Ezek. 36:25-27; cf. Mal. 3:1-3). This emphasis was Jeremiah's promise of the new covenant (Jer. 31:31-34), which the Epistle to the Hebrews declares to be now in full enactment (Heb. 10:14-17).

Through the blood of Christ offered for the sins of "the many," the guilt of sin is removed in justification (Matt. 26:27-28), and by the gift of the Holy Spirit, God writes his law on the fleshly tables of our hearts (2 Cor. 3) in a work of sanctification which is "both gradual and instantaneous" (Wesley). He who is "the Lord and Giver of Life"[14] is also "the Spirit of holiness," who in the new birth initiates the holiness that as cleansing is perfected in entire sanctification (2 Cor. 7:1) and that viewed positively is the progressive restoration of the image of God, by "the Lord who is the Spirit" (2 Cor. 3:18, RSV).

3. The Dual Meaning of Pentecost

In the light of the preceding, the dispensational promise of the Father—the baptism with the Holy Spirit—must be understood as both historic and experiential, initiatory and sanctifying.

a. Historically, the Pentecostal baptism with the Holy Spirit formed the church as Christ's Spirit-filled body, commissioned to continue his ministry of reconciliation in history (Acts 1:1).

On the day of Pentecost, the Holy Spirit came to *remain* with the church to the end of the age. "The Father . . . will give you another [Paraclete]," Jesus pledged the disciples in the Upper Room, "to abide with you forever" (John 14:16). Wesley comments, "With you, and your followers to the end of the age."[15] In this sense "the Spirit was not yet given" until Jesus was glorified (7:39, NASB). But now, "the Spirit and the gifts are ours" ("A Mighty Fortress Is Our God," Luther).

Strictly speaking, Pentecost is as truly an event of history as Bethlehem, and in a literal sense cannot be repeated. Pentecost was the birthday of the Christian church, the animating of a powerless group of believers into an energized, sanctified community, imbued not only as individuals but also as a corporate body with the powers of the Spirit. It created a *community* of saints, a *koinonia* of the Holy Spirit—the Holy Church.[16] Pentecost has been called "the incorporation of God" as Christmas is termed "the incarnation of God." Something was done on the first Whitsunday that was unique and unrepeatable: *the Spirit was given.*

> *Our glorified Head*
> *His Spirit has shed*
> *With His people to stay*
> *And never again will He take Him away.*
>
> —Charles Wesley

The Lukan statement that "they were *all* filled with the Holy Ghost" (Acts 2:4, emphasis added) refers dispensationally, therefore, to the *collective* filling of the church as Christ's body, "the fulness of him who fills all in all" (Eph. 1:23, RSV). On the day of Pentecost the church became the true temple of the Spirit (cf. 2:13-22); this theological idea is the one that illuminates the accounts of the Spirit's coming in Samaria (Acts 8:14-17), Joppa (10:44-46; 11:15), and Ephesus (19:6). By the Spirit given at Pentecost, these believers beyond Jerusalem were subsequently incorporated into the new body of Christ, the temple of the Spirit. The confirmatory sign of this baptism by the Spirit was water baptism, which signified the mystical divine incorporation but which bore no necessary time-relation to the Spirit's work (cf. Acts 19:5-6 with Acts 10:47-48). And "by one Spirit *we* were all baptized into one body—Jews or Greeks, slaves or free—and all were made to drink of one Spirit" (1 Cor. 12:13, RSV, emphasis added). To be a Christian is to be baptized—by the Spirit and water—into the body of Christ, the community of the Spirit. This involvement is to receive the gift of the Spirit (cf. Gal. 3:1-5, 13-14). So Paul can declare, "Any one who does not have the Spirit of Christ does not belong to him" (Rom. 8:9, RSV). And, conversely, he can say to the Colossians, "Christ is all, and in all" (Col. 3:11)—by the Spirit who fills his body. While this explanation by no means exhausts the meaning of Spirit baptism, it does define its initiatory sense.

b. The Spirit who came at Pentecost (and who comes to us who believe in Christ), however, is preeminently the sanctifying Spirit whose distinctive work in the eschaton is to purify the hearts of believers and perfect them in God's love, thus fulfilling the promise of the new covenant (Ezek. 36:25-27; Jer. 31:31-34). "He will baptize you with the Holy Spirit and with fire,"

John the Baptist announced (Matt. 3:11; Luke 3:16, RSV). John here echoes Malachi's pledge that the Messenger of the covenant should "purify the sons of Levi, and purge them as gold and silver" so that they might "offer unto the LORD an offering in righteousness" (Mal. 3:3). The fire of the Divine Messenger, however, would not only refine God's faithful servants but also burn up as stubble those who were arrogant and evildoers (4:1). John Calvin comments on Malachi's prophecy: "The power of fire is twofold, for it burns and it purifies; it burns up the corrupt but it purifies gold and silver from their dross. The prophet no doubt meant to include both."[17] John's prophecy has the same double reference.[18] "Every one will be salted with fire" (Mark 9:49, RSV), either the fire of Pentecost or the fire of Gehenna. God's holiness is a devouring fire, which will either purge away our sin or destroy us with it![19]

Heart holiness is therefore the climactic meaning of Christ's baptism with the Holy Spirit. "This," H. V. Miller rightly insists, "is the constant emphasis of the New Testament—the work, the presence, the purity, the power of the Holy Spirit." Miller continues,

> Dispensationally all was to climax in Him. His coming to the individual heart of the believer in purifying, empowering presence was the final fruition of the ages past. Not that He should receive the pre-eminence but that He might give it. It was to become His task to crystallize and conserve the work of Calvary . . . We live today in the dispensation of the Holy Spirit. He is the sovereignly chosen member of the Trinity to carry out the purposes of God in the earth. . . . His indwelling presence must be recognized and established as an experiential reality in the heart of everyone who would do the will of God.[20]

Pentecost, that is to say, is not only a historic gift of the Spirit; it is an experience to be *realized*, a promise of holiness and spiritual fullness to be *appropriated*. So Paul can pray for the Ephesians, who were "a dwelling place of God in the Spirit" (Eph. 2:22, RSV), that they might receive the inner strength of the promised Comforter and experience the full indwelling of Christ in their hearts, that they might "be filled to the measure of all the fullness of God" (Eph. 3:19, NIV). "Therefore do not be foolish, but understand what the Lord's will is," he later exhorts; "Do not get drunk on wine, which leads to debauchery. Instead, be filled with the Spirit" (5:17-18, NIV).

Therefore, at Christmas we sing, "O come to my heart, Lord Jesus, / There is room in my heart for Thee," and knowing the promise of the Spirit's sanctifying fullness, we can pray,

Refining fire, go through my heart,
Illuminate my soul.
Scatter Thy life through every part,
And sanctify the whole.
—Charles Wesley

Pentecost is a date to be commemorated: the birthday of the church when the Spirit was given. Pentecost is also the pledge of spiritual fullness and personal sanctity. That truth is expressed in these words:

When'er our day of Pentecost
Is fully come, we surely know
The Father, Son, and Holy Ghost
One God, is manifest below:
The Son doth in the Father dwell,
The Father in His Son imparts
His Spirit of joy unspeakable
And lives forever in our hearts.
—Charles Wesley

To safeguard the full biblical teaching of Spirit baptism, both the historic and personal aspects of Pentecost must be preserved. To neglect either is to destroy the beautiful balance of New Testament truth and distort the significance of the Father's promise.[21]

The Baptism with the Holy Spirit

At the risk of being repetitious, it must be said again that the baptism with the Holy Spirit is both historic and personal, corporate and individual, initiatory and sanctifying. The relationship between these two aspects is suggested by Paul in Romans: "Do you not know that all of us who have been baptized into Christ Jesus have been baptized into his death? We were buried therefore with him by baptism *into death*" (Rom. 6:3-4, RSV, emphasis added). Baptism into Christ is baptism into his death, a death to sin.

Luke records an interesting exclamation of Jesus that touches on this issue: "I came to cast fire upon the earth; and would that it were already kindled! I have a baptism to be baptized with; and how I am constrained until it is accomplished!" (Luke 12:49-50, RSV). Before he could administer his fiery baptism, Jesus must be "baptized" into his atoning death! (cf. John 7:39). Moreover, it was in view of this death that Jesus had submitted to baptism in the Jordan at the outset of his ministry. That signal event must be understood as both the Father's identification of Jesus as the messianic Son and also as our Lord's self-conscious dedication to his work as the Suffering Servant whose mission was to suffer and die for the sins of "the many."[22] Jesus' water baptism was the prefigurement of the saving "baptism" of his death on the cross. To put it differently, his baptism was *baptism into death* (cf. Mark 10:38-45).

Likewise, Christian baptism is baptism into death. To be baptized into Christ is to be baptized into *his* death: "We were buried therefore with him by baptism [with the Spirit and water] into death" (Rom. 6:4, RSV). Paul's argument is unmistakably clear: to be a baptized Christian is to have undergone with him a death to sin, which must now be *realized* in the pervasive sanctification of our existence. Baptism into Christ is baptism into his death, which both promises (v. 11) and obligates (vv. 12-13) the believer to experience the deeper crisis of full sanctification (v. 19).

While most commentators see in 1 Cor. 12:13 a reference only to the initiatory baptism of the Spirit, Dr. Wiley observes rightly that Paul's argument also requires the deeper meaning of entire sanctification.[23] The apostle's theme in 1 Cor. 12 is the unity of Christ's body, which was the burden of Jesus' High Priestly Prayer for the church: "Sanctify them . . . that they may all be one . . . that the love with which thou hast loved me may be in them, and I in them" (John 17:17, 21, 26, RSV). The baptism that incorporates us into Christ is not truly accomplished until it purges us from the sinful self-bias of our hearts and dyes us in the Christlike love Paul extols in 1 Cor. 13.

It was the glory of the Protestant Reformation that it recovered for the church the meaning of personal salvation: to be Christian was no longer a matter of institutional membership but of personal trust in Christ. However, under the constant influence of Renaissance thinking, in due time the pendulum swung to the opposite extreme of atomistic individualism: to be Christian became a matter entirely of individual experience, with the church becoming merely incidental to spiritual life. The biblical understanding of the church and the sacraments dissolved in the acids of Enlightenment thought. More than we probably are ready to acknowledge, our contemporary Protestant ideas of the Spirit's work bear the impress of such rationalistic individualism.

Have we given due weight to the New Testament body of Christ setting of the Spirit's work of sanctification? Have we really understood Wesley's insistence that New Testament holiness is *social* holiness? "'Holy solitaries' is a phrase no more consistent with the Gospel than holy adulterers," Wesley argued. "The Gospel of Christ knows no religion, but social; no holiness, but social holiness" (from the preface to *Poetical Works of John and Charles Wesley*). Sanctification by the Spirit occurs only in "the community of the saints." That fact is why Wesley organized his followers into societies and classes and bands and insisted that they constantly attend Holy Communion and all the public means of grace. Perfect love is the gift of the Spirit only in the body of Christ.

Is the baptism with the Holy Spirit initiatory or sanctifying? To make this matter an either/or one is to put asunder what God has evidently joined together. We Wesleyans dare not become polarized by two emphases that are equally valid New Testament teachings. A synthesis of these two concepts would seem to offer a basis for strengthening our theological position, preserving on the one hand our distinctively Wesleyan message and providing on the other a more satisfying position for those who are concerned to "do" theology biblically. At the same time, this approach provides a hermeneutical principle that will permit our holiness theology to offer correctives to popular body-life teachings, which tend to sever the Spirit's charismatic bestowments from his sanctifying activity.

VI
SANCTIFICATION AND THE
CHRISTUS VICTOR MOTIF IN
WESLEYAN THEOLOGY

———— ✺ ————

This essay was published in the Wesleyan Theological Journal, in 1972 and with slight modification and addition again in 2003. It represents Dr. Greathouse's career-long emphasis on the atonement as it relates to the Wesleyan understanding of sanctification. Although he believed there were other elements involved, this theme was his major emphasis. The essay also demonstrates how he believed this teaching should be integrated into the entire scope of Christian theology. Another very interesting feature appears in footnote 21. Dr. Greathouse has adopted the view considered by some (including H. Orton Wiley) as heretical, namely, in the incarnation the Son assumed "fallen human nature." [With that conclusion this editor fully concurs. HRD]

GUSTAF AULEN'S *Christus Victor*[1] ranks as one of the most influential works on the atonement to appear in our time. Aulen calls for a thorough revision of the traditional account of the history of the idea of the atonement to give fresh emphasis to a view of Christ's work, which he describes as the "dramatic" motif. Its central theme is the idea of the atonement as a divine conflict and victory in which Christ—*Christus Victor*—enlists and vanquishes Satan, sin, and death.[2] He insists that this dramatic understanding of Christ's work is a true doctrine of atonement because in this act God reconciles the world to himself.[3] Although Christ's death is at the heart of redemption, the cross presupposes the incarnation, for it was the Son of God in the flesh who met and vanquished evil.[4] It also embraces the resurrection and ascension, for by raising his Son from the dead to his own right hand God fulfilled the conditions for the promised gift of the Spirit by which Christ's historic victory is mediated to believers.[5] The cross also envisions the consummation of redemption when God will send his Son a second time to raise and glorify us with him.[6]

The "Classic" Idea of Atonement

The *Christus Victor* view of Christ's work Aulen calls "the classic idea" of the atonement. He sees it as the dominant idea of the New Testament.[7] Thus it did not spring into being in the early church or arrive as an importation from some outside source. It was, in fact, the ruling idea of the atonement for the first thousand years of Christian history. In the Middle Ages it was gradually ousted from its place in the theological teaching of the church, but it survived still in her devotional language and art. It confronts us again, more vigorously and profoundly expressed than ever before, in Martin Luther, and it constituted an important part of his expression of the Christian faith. It has, therefore, every right to claim the title of the classic idea of the atonement.[8]

Aulen has done the church a service in rescuing the dramatic view of Christ's work and restoring it to its rightful place as a New Testament account of the atonement. In the traditional understanding of the history of the idea of the atonement, the *Christus Victor* teaching has been slighted, if not rejected outright, along with the ransom theory, which grew out of it.[9] Aulen shows how the New Testament does indeed see Christ's work as a divine conquest of evil. Moreover, he seems to have successfully demonstrated that this is a view of atonement and not merely a doctrine of salvation. Furthermore, this representation of Christ's redemptive work preserves the biblical teaching that the atonement is from beginning to end the work of God (2 Cor. 5:18). It also dynamically fuses the objective and subjective features of this work. Such a viewpoint provides a sound basis for pointing up weaknesses in both the Anselmic and Abelardian theories.

It may be questioned, however, whether any one view of the atonement can be rightly titled *classic*. The New Testament regards Christ's work in at least three ways: as propitiation, as redemption, and as reconciliation. As sinners, we are guilty and exposed to the wrath of God; in Christ, God propitiates his wrath and expiates our guilt. As sinners we are in bondage to Satan and sin; Christ's redemptive act delivers us from bondage and sets us at liberty. As sinners we are alienated and estranged from God; we are reconciled to God by the death of his Son. The *Christus Victor* motif elucidates the second representation of atonement. While Aulen maintains that the other two ideas may be fully subsumed under this one view,[10] it may be questioned that the dramatic motif adequately embraces the notions of propitiation and reconciliation. Strong biblical and experiential reasons seem to have given rise to the emphases of Anselm and Abelard. A truly classic doctrine of atonement includes both the ideas of satisfaction and of revelation as well as of that of redemption. Whatever weaknesses we may find in the Anselmic and Abelardian theories, we cannot deny that they voice two distinct scriptural perspectives. It is a question whether these viewpoints can be fully expressed in the *Christus Victor* doctrine.

In spite of these questions, *Christus Victor* is a view of Christ's work that highlights the atonement as the destruction of sin that makes possible true sanctification and perfection. While it may be too much to claim that it provides the entire framework for explaining Christ's work, it does give Wesleyan theology a significant biblical and historical basis for developing a thoroughgoing christological doctrine of sanctification. The *Christus Victor* idea "directs attention not primarily to the punishment and the other consequences of sin, but to sin itself. It is sin itself which is overcome by Christ, and annihilated; it is from the power of sin itself that man is set free."[11] In Christ God has sanctified the race; this sanctification is accomplished within us as Christ comes to indwell us in the Spirit. Aulen further spells out the implication of this interpretation: "The classic idea of salvation is that the victory which Christ gained once for all is continued in the work of the Holy Spirit, and its fruits reaped."[12]

Christ's Victory for Us

The atonement has several facets. Viewed from the standpoint of human guilt and our deep need for pardon and acceptance, Christ crucified is God's perfect oblation, making possible our justification (Rom. 3:21-26; 1 Cor. 1:30*b*). Seen from the perspective of our enmity toward God and our profound yearning for restored fellowship, Christ provides reconciliation (2

Cor. 5:14-21; Eph. 2:11-22). Again, perceived from the angle of humankind's bondage to evil, Christ crucified is the conqueror of Satan, sin, and death. It is this third point of view—*Christus Victor*—which Aulen sees as dominant until Anselm, and it is this understanding of Christ's work that furnishes the most solid basis for a dynamic biblical doctrine of sanctification.

This view presupposes that it was only by meeting the forces of evil on their own ground, only, that is, by getting into history where they were entrenched, that Christ could break their power.[13] He partook of flesh and blood that through death he might destroy him who had the power of death, that is, the devil (Heb. 2:13-14). In his final effort to destroy the Prince of Life (Jesus Christ), the devil overextended and thus defeated himself (John 12:31; cf. 16:11; 1 Cor. 2:6 and 1 John 2:8). God the Father "disarmed the principalities and powers and made a public example of them, triumphing over them in him [Christ]" (Col. 2:15, RSV).

Christus Victor, moreover, not only defeated Satan; he destroyed sin itself: "The reason the Son of God appeared was to destroy the works of the devil" (1 John 3:8, RSV). John means that Christ came to destroy the principle of lawlessness (*anomian*—1 John 3:4), which was the devil's chief work in humankind.

Paul gives the fullest treatment of sanctification within the context of Romans 5:12—8:39. Particularly critical to this idea are Romans 6:6 and 8:3. First, Romans 6:6—"Knowing this, that our old man is crucified with him, that the body of sin might be destroyed, that henceforth we should not serve sin." Knowing what? We know that in and with the death of Jesus on Calvary we were provisionally crucified also, so that we might be delivered from sin for a life of love service to God. Paul puts the same idea slightly differently in 2 Corinthians—"For the love of Christ controls us, because we are convinced that one has died for all; therefore all have died. And he died for all, that those who live might live no longer for themselves but for him who for their sake died and was raised" (5:14-15, RSV).

Two definitions are in order with reference to Romans 6:6: "our old man" (*ho palaios hemen anthropos*) and "the body of sin" (*to soma tes hamartias*). The first expression must be understood in the light of Romans 5:12-14; the second, of Romans 7:14-25. Both must be defined in terms of these two contexts. Here are two concepts that describe different aspects of human sinfulness. "Our old man" is therefore "Adam and ourselves in Adam."[14] "The body of sin" should be taken as the possessive genitive: "sin's body," or "the body of which sin has taken possession, 'i.e. body that is so apt to be the instrument of its own carnal impulses.'"[15] Indwelt by sin (*he hamartia*),[16] I am hopelessly divided against myself and reduced to moral impotence (Rom. 7:14-25). Paul's other term for this sin-dominated body is "flesh" (*sarx*— Rom. 7:18; cf. 8:8).[17]

Now, Paul says, "Our old man was crucified with Christ, so that sin's body [i.e., *sarx*, the flesh] might be destroyed, that henceforth we might not be enslaved by sin" (Rom. 6:6). Karl Barth vividly paraphrases Paul:

> This is our knowledge of Jesus Christ on which our faith is founded— that the "old man" (i.e., we ourselves as God's enemies) have been cruci- fied and killed in and with the crucifixion of the man Jesus at Golgotha so that the "body" (i.e., the subject, the person needed for the doing) of sin, the man who can sin and will sin and shall sin has been removed, destroyed, done away with, is simply no longer there (and has therefore not merely been "made powerless").[18]

Whatever Barth may allow by this explanation, his words give true expres- sion of Paul's declaration. As a new man in Christ, I am to hear the gospel saying to me that my old self in Adam has been crucified with Christ in order that my total person may be liberated from sin, so that I may serve God in "righteousness for sanctification" (Rom. 6:19, RSV). That statement is the whole meaning of Romans 6.

Romans 8:3 relates this meaning to the incarnation. Christ's victory could be won only in the flesh. But there, where sin had established its rule, *Christus Victor* routed it decisively: "For God has done what the law, weakened by the flesh, could not do: by sending his own Son in the likeness of sinful flesh ['sin's flesh' or 'sin-dominated flesh'], and to deal with sin, he condemned sin in the flesh" (NRSV). *Condemned* means more than to register disapproval; the law accomplishes disapproval. Christ pronounced the doom of sin. Sin was henceforth "deposed from its autocratic power."[19] "By his life of perfect obedience, and his victorious death and resurrection," C. H. Dodd comments, "the reign of sin over human nature has been bro- ken."[20] The Son of God "'condemned' that 'sin' which was 'in' our 'flesh,'" Wesley asserts, "gave sentence that sin should be destroyed and the believer wholly delivered from it" (Rom. 8:3, *Explanatory Notes*). On the very ground where sin had established itself—in human flesh—the Son of God has vanquished sin and potentially sanctified our human existence!

Christ's Victory in Us

Christ's victory *for* us becomes his victory *in* us by the indwelling Spirit (Rom. 8:1-11). Christ's victory is reproduced in us. In the Holy Spirit, Christ for us becomes Christ in us, recapitulating in our history his triumph over sin. This inner conquest is the meaning of *Christus Victor* for sanctification.[21]

Every demon we meet is foredoomed in Christ. Sin itself has lost its power for the believer in whom Christ dwells: "Little children, you are of God, and have overcome them; for He who is in you is greater than he who is in the world. . . . and this is the victory that overcomes the world, our faith. . . . We know that any one born of God does not sin, but He who was born of God keeps him, and the evil one does not touch him" (1 John 4:4; 5:4, 18 RSV).

This victory is given to us in three stages—in conversion, in entire sanctification, and in glorification. Victory over sin begins in conversion. This implication is the clear teaching of Romans 6:1-11. It is our knowledge of the gospel—that we ourselves have been crucified in the person of Christ crucified. Paul insists that we grasp the truth that our crucifixion has already happened to us "in principle" in our justification and regeneration: "For he who has died is freed from sin" (v. 7, RSV). But in order to reap the full benefits of God's provision, we must furnish what Godet calls "moral cooperation." "The believer understands that the final object which God has in view in crucifying [the] old man (v. 6) is to realize . . . the life of the Risen One (vv. 8, 9), and he enters actively into the divine thought."[22]

To enter "actively into the divine thought" and thereby realize true sanctification involves the following: (1) a faith knowledge that God has actually accomplished the destruction of sin in Christ crucified and resurrected and that in my conversion I have embraced his death to sin and with him have been raised to "newness of life" in which I am no longer sin's slave, and (2) a complete break with sin (Rom. 6:12-13a) and a putting of myself absolutely at God's disposal in a critical act of consecration (vv. 13a, 19) so that I may begin to realize the full life of the risen Lord in me.

We have already provisionally died with Christ through our participation in his crucifixion; now we must permit that death to reach to the very depths of our being as we cease from self and begin to live wholly to God. The death of the "old man" is thus a process initiated by conversion and realized in entire sanctification. "In principle" we die with Christ in justification; in full reality, we die with him when we yield up ourselves to God as Jesus gave up his spirit to the Father on the cross. Here John Wesley has a guiding word:

> A man may be dying for some time; yet he does not, properly speaking, die, till the soul is separated from the body; and in that instant, he lives the life of eternity. In like manner, he may be dying to sin for some time; yet he is not dead to sin till it is separated from his soul; and in that instant, he lives the full life of love. So the change wrought when the soul died to sin is of a different kind and infinitely greater than any before, and than he can conceive, till he experiences it. Yet he still grows in grace, and in the knowledge of Christ, in the love and image of God; and will do so, not only till death, but to all eternity.[23]

Christ's victory thus becomes blessed reality in entire sanctification, in the perfecting of our love. This separation of the soul from sin to God is the final object God has in mind in crucifying the old man (Rom. 6). Viewed positively, this act of God is life in the Spirit (Rom. 8). Christ reenacts in us the sanctification he accomplished in the atonement. By his perfect obedience and victorious death and resurrection he provisionally expelled sin from human experience; now he comes in the Spirit to dwell and reign in us and thereby work in us the loving obedience that fulfills the "just requirement" of the law (Rom. 8:4—Gk. *dikaioma*). Thus, Christ himself becomes our sanctification (1 Cor. 1:30c): "For in him the whole fulness of deity dwells bodily, and you have come to fulness of life in him" (Col. 2:9-10, RSV). This fullness, however, is not a private, mystical, quietistic union with Christ. It is social; it is life in the body of Christ (1 Cor. 12:12-27; Eph. 2:21—2:7; 4:4-16; Col. 3:1-4, 11-17; cf. Heb. 2:10-13). In the body of Christ—the *koinonia* of the Spirit—we discover the full meaning of "Christ in you, the hope of glory" (Col. 1:27; see vv. 21-29).

To put the matter in fullest perspective, we must add one further word. Christ's victory is complete but not final. We have been "saved in hope"—

the hope of resurrection and glorification with Christ (Rom. 8:17-15; 1 Cor. 15:22-28; Phil. 3:12-21). Meanwhile our sanctification has the character of spiritual warfare in which our victory over sin is assured as we permit Christ to live moment by moment in us (John 15:1-6; Eph. 6:10-15; Phil. 1:6; Col. 1:18-23; Rom. 8:12-13, 26-39; 13:11-14; Heb. 7:25). This victory is the practical meaning of *Christus Victor* for a theology of holiness. "Thanks be to God, who gives us the victory through our Lord Jesus Christ" (1 Cor. 15:57, RSV)—over the dominion of sin in conversion, over sin itself in sanctification, over the racial consequences of sin in glorification.

Wesley and *Christus Victor*

John Deschner has pointed out the relevance of *Christus Victor* for Wesley's doctrine of sanctification:

> The grand theme of Wesleyan Atonement is Christ's bearing our guilt and punishment on the cross. This atonement is Wesley's ground for man's entire salvation, his sanctification as well as his justification. However, alongside this judicial scheme of thought, there is also in Wesley a pervasive tendency to view Christ's work on Good Friday and Easter, but also today and in the future, in terms of a military victory for us over sin and evil. Much attention has been given to the power of the Holy Spirit in Wesley's doctrine of sanctification. It needs to be more clearly recognized that the sanctifying Spirit is the Spirit of the victorious as well as the suffering Christ.[24]

Wesley's *Explanatory Notes upon the New Testament* make it abundantly clear that he both knew and appreciated the *Christus Victor* idea, and three of his Standard Sermons have this theme.[25] However, Wesley does not take full advantage of the implications of this view for his doctrine of holiness. "It may well be that this is a weakness in his doctrine of sanctification," Colin Williams observes. "There is a stress on a conscious individual relationship with Christ, and little emphasis is given to the need for the repetition of Christ's victory in us."[26] Such a view of sanctification, however, is present in Wesley, although it is not consistently pressed.

Other elements of Wesley's thought rival this idea and thereby rob Wesley's doctrine of the Christocentricity that marks the New Testament teaching of sanctification. A clarification of Wesleyan theology at this point should give new power and relevance to its holiness teaching.

In his *Notes* Wesley affirms, as we have seen, that God has given sentence "that sin should be destroyed, and the believer wholly delivered from it" (on Rom. 8:3).[27] He comments, "The Son of God was manifested to destroy the works of the devil—all sin. And will he not perform this in all who trust in him?" (on 1 John 3:8). In his sermon on this latter text, however, Wesley limits the manifestation of Christ to the "inward manifestation of himself."[28] Not once in this entire sermon does he refer to Christ's objective victory on the cross, although he makes passing reference to Christ's final victory in the last day. By ignoring the objective victory of Christ, Wesley opens the door to a subjective, individualistic type of holiness. The message of sanctification would have been more vigorously positive and biblical if he had sounded with clarity the note of Christ's historic conquest of sin.

Moreover, because Wesley does not seem to see clearly that sanctification is the repetition of Christ's victory in us, Deschner thinks, it is "not primarily a participation in Christ who, as Paul says, is also our sanctification (1 Corinthians 1:30), but rather such a relation to Christ as allows His Spirit to establish in us a 'temper,' a more abstract stylized kind of holiness."[29] In the light of recent studies of Wesley's psychology, with the attendant emphasis on the importance of the means of grace in the development of holy character, Deschner's criticism of Wesley may be too strong.[30] What it appears he is pointing out is that holiness is only *secondarily* a "habitus"—a psychological habit-pattern; it is *primarily* the indwelling of Christ within, a position Wesley would endorse. And what is "righteousness," Wesley asks, "but the life of God in the soul; the mind which was in Christ Jesus; the image of God stamped upon the heart, now renewed after the image of him that created it?"[31] The latter pages of his *Plain Account* suggest that Wesley had indeed come to see the sanctifying Spirit as the Spirit of the victorious as well as the suffering Christ, in Christ's role as Prophet, Priest, and King. Listen to the mature Wesley:

> The holiest of men still need Christ, as their Prophet, as "the light of the world." For he does not give them light, but from moment to moment; the instant he withdraws, all is darkness. They still need Christ as their King; for God does not give them a stock of holiness. But unless they

receive a supply every moment, nothing but unholiness would remain. They still need Christ as their Priest, to make atonement for their holy things. Even perfect holiness is acceptable to God only through Jesus Christ. . . . The best of men may therefore say, "Thou art my light, my holiness, my heaven. Through my union with Thee, I am full of light, of holiness, and happiness. But if I were left to myself I should be nothing but sin, darkness, hell."[32]

This explanation is Wesley at his best. Here he means by perfection, not simply any "temper," "intention," or "affection" inherent in man himself, but a participation in the being of Christ's love. Christ is both the content and source of this perfection. On the ground of Christ's priestly work, the prophetic and kingly offices can also be understood as grace.

We can only regret that Wesley, having suggested such an exalted view of Christ's intercession, did not fully articulate it in his doctrine of sanctification. We are not "holy in Christ" (as Wesley abhorred), but "in Christ" we are actually made holy. Here he could have found his sound defense against antinomianism (Heb. 7:25). And it can be argued that statement was, in the band societies, Wesley's pastoral answer to antinomianism. There his Methodists found their place in the body of Christ with its worship, exhortation, admonition, encouragement, and service. There they experienced the presence and power of Christ who had won for them the victory. Though Wesley may not have done so, must we not develop this doctrine's implication that we participate in Christ's active righteousness, through the Holy Spirit, in the church, which is his body? Perhaps we are being called upon to restore Wesley's insistence upon the means of grace *as an essential ingredient of the doctrine of sanctification.*

For believers awaiting God's promise of "entire renewal in the image of God," it is necessary that they wait for this fulfillment, says Wesley:

Not in careless indifference, or indolent inactivity; but in vigorous, universal obedience, in a zealous keeping of all the commandments, in watchfulness and painfulness, in denying ourselves, and taking up our cross daily; as well as in earnest prayer and fasting, and a close attendance on all the ordinances of God. And if any man dream of attaining it any other way (yea, or of keeping it when it is attained, when he has received it even in the largest measure), he deceiveth his own soul. It is true, we receive it by simple faith: But God does not, will not, give that faith, unless we seek it with all diligence, in the way which he hath ordained.[33]

Fallen creatures, lifted up by God's grace, can remain in that grace, Wesley was convinced, only when they appropriate it in obedience to his commandments. And we can grow in that grace, he insisted, only by constant attendance upon the means of grace, which if we neglect leads to that falling away which is the occasion of sin. "By 'means of grace,'" he explained, "I understand outward signs, words, or actions, ordained by God, and appointed for this end, to be the ordinary channels whereby He might convey to men, preventing, justifying, or sanctifying grace."[34]

Whatever deficiency we may find in John Wesley's appropriation of the *Christus Victor* idea in his theological formulation of the doctrine of sanctification, we still have much to learn from his practical theology if we are to keep the message of holiness pertinent and alive in these times. In the final analysis, Christian perfection is the *worship* of God in the beauty of holiness. The challenge we face is the development of a full-orbed formulation of Wesley's theology that does justice to the *Christus Victor* idea, as at the same time we reconnect the means of grace to the end for which we were created—to be holy, even as God is holy.

VII
SIN: A WESLEYAN DEFINITION

This article appeared in Illustrated Bible Life, *June-August 1998. It reflects an emphasis of Wesleyan theology that Dr. Greathouse highlighted often. The early holiness movement of the nineteenth century had, in its enthusiasm for the "second blessing," frequently fallen into the trap of "perfectionism." As a result, many sensitive persons were disillusioned and/or depressed over the fact that their experience did not conform to such extravagant claims. It was Dr. Greathouse's purpose by his emphasis to both adequately reflect his Wesleyan commitment and to speak realistically about life lived under the conditions of finite and fallen existence.*

THE PROPER PLACE to begin an exploration of the unique Wesleyan definition of sin is John's declaration, "No one who is born of God will continue to sin, because God's seed remains in them; they cannot go on sinning, because they have been born of God" (1 John 3:9, NIV). This conviction was central in Wesley's gospel. "Even babes in Christ," he wrote, "are so far perfect as not to commit sin."[1]

A Proper Definition of Sin

But what does it mean "not to commit sin"? We find our answer in verse 4: "Everyone who sins breaks the law; in fact, sin is lawlessness" (NIV). For this text, Wesley draws his well-known definition: "A proper definition of sin is a voluntary transgression of a known law of God."[2] Although Wesley's definition is not quite as simple as the foregoing statement seems to imply, it is the place to begin our exploration.

A Sinning Saint?

For Wesley, the expression "sinning saint" was a moral contradiction, like "truthful liar," "honest crook," or "virtuous harlot"! He did recognize the possibility of "sins of surprise," when in an unguarded moment we may say or do something that displeases God. Immediately confessed and forsaken, he taught, such sins may be forgiven without rupturing our relationship with Christ. But such failures are like a train wreck—they are not on the schedule! By the grace of God, we *need not* sin (see 1 John 2:1-6)

Wesley found preposterous the Calvinistic notion that Christ's righteousness is like an umbrella, hiding a justified believer from God's sight, providing forgiveness for all our sins "past, present, *and future*." Referring to Romans 4:1-8, he insisted, "Least of all does justification imply, that God is deceived in those whom he justifies; that he thinks them to be what, in fact, they are not."[3] God always sees us as we truly are, and John states, "But if we walk in the light as He is in the light, . . . the blood of Jesus Christ His Son cleanses us from all sin" (1 John 1:7, NKJV).

Furthermore, at the very moment God *justifies* us through Christ, he begins to *sanctify* us through the Holy Spirit.[4]

The Law of Christ

Thus, while the new birth effects in us a *moral* change, Wesley's thought is not moralistic or legalistic. To a Mrs. Bennis struggling with her human weaknesses, he wrote, "Every voluntary breach of *the law of love* is sin; and nothing else, if we speak properly . . . Let love fill your heart, and it is enough!"[5] Agreeing with Paul, he taught that "love is the fulfilling of the law" (Rom. 13:10). For him, all the commandments are comprehended in the one commandment to love God and neighbor (Matt. 22:37-40). The law of Christ is *the law of love*.

"Faith Expressing Itself through Love"

For many years, I have taught ministers in college and seminary. I enjoy asking a class, "How many of you can stand to your feet and recite the Ten Commandments?" An embarrassing moment usually follows. After chiding them a bit, I say, "Don't be embarrassed. The wonder of the gospel is that when we believe, God *writes his law in our hearts* by his Spirit, so that we are enabled spontaneously to obey commandments we may not be able to recite" (see 2 Cor. 3). John states that idea in this way: "This is the love of God, that we keep his commandments. And his commandments are not burdensome" (1 John 5:3, RSV). "Faith expressing itself through love" is the essence of Wesley's gospel (Gal. 5:6, NIV). Of justification by faith, Luther writes, "The Spirit makes the heart glad and free, as the law requires that it shall be."[6] Here Luther and Wesley agree.

Commenting on 1 John 3:9 (KJV), Wesley writes,

Whoever is born of God, by a living faith, whereby God is continually breathing spiritual life into his soul, and his soul is continually breathing out love and prayer to God, *doth not commit sin.* For the divine seed of loving faith *abideth in him; and*, so long as it doth, *he cannot sin, because he is born of God*—is inwardly and universally changed.[7]

Such an understanding of our relationship to God is at the opposite pole from loveless legalism. The revealed secret of victory over sin is the following: "But you, dear friends, by building yourselves up in your most holy faith and praying in the Holy Spirit, keep yourselves in God's love as you wait for the mercy of our Lord Jesus Christ to bring you to eternal life" (Jude vv. 20-21, NIV). Such an admonition breathes the spirit of Wesley's gospel.

"Sin Improperly So Called"

Thus far we have considered what Wesley called "sin properly so called"—conscious, willful sin. But Wesley recognized what he called, for want of a better term, "sin improperly so called." "I believe there is no such perfection in life that excludes these involuntary transgressions which I apprehend to be naturally consequent on the ignorance and mistakes inseparable from humanity," he writes. "Therefore *sinless perfection* is a phrase I never use, lest I seem to contradict myself. I believe a person filled with love is still liable to these transgressions."[8]

A few pages later, he gives a careful exposition of 1 Corinthians 13. Then he writes, "You who feel nothing but love compare yourselves with the preceding description. Weigh yourselves in this balance and see if you are not wanting in many particulars."[9] Even those who enjoy "love made perfect," he taught, fall short of "the perfect law" of God. Therefore, he wants us to know, "The best of [persons] need Christ as their Priest, their

Atonement, their Advocate with the Father; not only as the continuance of their every blessing depends on His death, but on account of their coming short of the law of love."[10] Everyone who understands the gospel confesses with Charles Wesley,

> Every moment, Lord, I need
> The merit of Thy death.

And when we come to die, we can only say with John Wesley: "What have I to trust to for salvation? I see nothing which I have done or suffered that bears looking at. I have no other plea than this,

> I the chief of sinners am,
> But Jesus died for me!"

St. Paul concludes, "It is because of [God] that you are in Christ Jesus, who has become for us wisdom from God—that is, our righteousness, holiness and redemption. Therefore, as it is written: 'Let him who boasts boast in the Lord'" (1 Cor. 1:30-31, NIV).[11]

VIII
THE DYNAMICS OF SANCTIFICATION: BIBLICAL TERMINOLOGY

———∞∞∞———

This paper was presented at a midquadrennial Nazarene Theology Conference in December 1969. It reflects his work on the book of Romans in the Beacon Bible Commentary that was published the preceding year. It appears at the time in the history of the holiness movement when the "folk theology" of the nineteenth century was beginning to be questioned by both the outsider as well as the insider. It is an attempt to ground the message soundly in Scripture as interpreted by the best of contemporary biblical scholarship.

THROUGH Georgia Harkness's spectacles, we can gain an outsider's view of us within the holiness movement. She writes bitingly,

> Sanctification with its correlative term "holiness" . . . is in bad odor today. Those of an older generation (and possibly not so old) who have heard those of the "holiness" sects talk about their "entire sanctification," claiming a self-righteous superiority in their victory over sin which others fail to see manifest in their lives, will have no truck with either term. . . . If we add to "sanctification" and "holiness" a third term, "Christian perfection," the rout is apt to be complete.[1]

While we detect in Harkness's observation a not-too-subtle perversion of Wesleyan teaching,[2] who can say it is totally unfair? Has not much popular holiness preachment abetted this erroneous view of sanctificationist doctrine? Our bland "folk theology" strongly tends toward semi-Pelagianism and strikes sensitive hearers as humanistic moralism. And, we sadly confess, it frequently lapses into outright legalism, which by its casuistry and ethical insensitivity does indeed reek with Pharisaism. By its lack of broad and deep biblical grounding, it has reduced the many-splendored scriptural truth of sanctification to simply "the second blessing" understood as a sort of watertight "experience" that will keep us secure until Christ returns to gather up the little flock of holiness professors.

Not only this perversion, but following a certain psychological methodology has surely detoured many around that deep and solitary death to sin that is the prerequisite to sanctifying faith.[3] When this detour takes place, emotional release replaces the Spirit's infilling. The sad result is institutional holiness—a doctrine of sanctification rather than the dynamic presence of the indwelling, sanctifying Spirit. Add to this outcome a hesitancy to admit the relevancy of the fact that, though Spirit-filled and cleansed, the holy still have their Christian existence in unredeemed bodies of mortal flesh, and the rout is indeed apt to be complete.[4]

This development, however, is only one side of the coin. As William Hordern reminds us, there is a new concern with sanctification among contemporary theologians.[5] Hordern is even able to claim that the late Karl Barth has developed "one of the most extensive treatments of sanctification since the work of John Wesley."[6] But Barth does not stand alone; evident in many current thinkers, both Protestant and Roman Catholic, is a new openness and honesty in biblical exegesis and exposition with respect to holiness.[7] While it is claiming too much to say that these men are articulating sanctification precisely in Wesleyan terms, the whole climate of biblical scholarship is surely conducive to positive dialogue.

Scholarly interest in Wesley also continues to the present time. In a recent volume, Robert E. Chiles has called upon his fellow Methodists to consider how far their theology has departed from the biblical and evangelical position of John Wesley.[8]

Nor should we overlook the growing realization, in evangelical circles outside the holiness movement, of the urgent need for the believer's being cleansed and filled with the Holy Spirit, an emphasis strikingly evident at the recent U.S. Congress on Evangelism. A renewed interest in the person and work of the Holy Spirit is present across a broad spectrum of theological orientations.

In view of factors it is urgent that we understand clearly our own theological position at all times. We must responsibly but courageously seek to correct the unscriptural and misleading emphases of "folk theology" in order to effect change toward a more dynamic, biblical, honest theology of sanctification.

What are the elements of such a theology of sanctification?

First, it must be evangelical—that is, developed in organic relationship to the doctrines of sin and grace. As Wesley insisted, the doctrine of original sin distinguishes Christianity as a revealed religion. It means that fallen man is totally incapable of himself to turn to God and be saved. His only hope is the prevenient grace of God. In the Nazarene Article of Faith on "Free Agency," the doctrine of human freedom is qualified by confessing "that through the fall of Adam (man) became depraved so that he cannot now turn and prepare himself by his own natural strength to faith and calling upon God."[9]

Here indeed is the Shibboleth.[10] If fallen man can of himself turn to God, "he has whereof to glory, but not before God." From first to last, our sanctification is *sola gratia, sola fide*.[11]

Original sin and Christian perfection must be kept in closest relationship, as Romans 5:12-21 shows. Wesleyanism rises to the heights of Pauline proclamation in matching the pessimistic doctrine of original sin with the optimistic announcement of abounding grace through Christ. It heralds this grace as universal in scope and sufficient in power to expel from the human heart the sin that entered through Adam's defection.[12]

Second, a dynamic theology of sanctification is *theocentric*. It begins with God and centers in God, who alone is holy in the absolute, unqualified sense and from whom alone our sanctification proceeds (Mark 10:18-27).

In simple terms, God is God (Isa. 42:8; 43:9-12). He is separated by "an infinitely qualitative chasm" from all he has created (Kierkegaard); the "Wholly other" (Otto), separate or "different" (William Barclay), the incomparable One (Isa. 40:24; cf. Amos 4:2; 6:8). He is all-glorious (Isa. 6:3; cf. Exod. 3:2-6). He is absolute purity, in whose presence man is struck with awe and the conviction of his own sinfulness.[13]

a. God's holiness defines sin—as the perverse attempt of the creature to bridge the chasm between himself and God (1) by imitating God's power and creativity in the false assertion of independence from God[14] or (2) by mimicking God's holiness in the pride of self-righteousness.[15] In both forms, it is man's unbelief and prideful self-sufficiency.

b. God's holiness defines redemption and sanctification. If sin is the perverse effort of man to build his Tower of Babel and reach heaven by his own scientific, philosophical, or religious ingenuity (see Gen. 11:4), redemption, with the resultant sanctification of man's existence, is accomplished *from above by God himself.*[16] God alone can bridge the unbridgeable chasm between himself and man, and this connecting he has done through Jesus Christ.

(1) Sanctification means basically that God separates a people to himself through the redemption that is in Christ Jesus.[17] A basic holiness text in the New Testament, therefore, is found in First Peter: "But you are a chosen race, a royal priesthood, a holy nation, God's own people, that you may declare the wonderful deeds of him who called you out of darkness into his marvelous light" (1 Pet. 2:9, RSV).[18] The "saints" are thus "the *Ecclesia* of God" (constituted by the gospel call which they have accepted in repentance, faith, and obedience), "the elect in Christ Jesus." They are those who have been "called to belong to Jesus Christ" (Rom. 1:6, RSV), and are hence "sanctified in Christ Jesus, saints by way of calling" (1 Cor. 1:2, literal rendering). This religious or cultic aspect of sanctification must ever be kept prior in our thought and teaching if we are to safeguard our theology from moralism and legalism. As egocentricity is the root of all sin, theocentricity is the root of all holiness.

(2) The people God calls and separates to himself through Christ's redemptive passion he purifies from sin (Titus 2:11-15). This moral meaning of sanctification was not immediately apparent in the earlier portions of the Old Testament revelation, where the ethical was often symbolized or typified by the ceremonial.[19] But as the Old Testament revelation unfolded, the religious meaning of sanctification was gradually filled with moral and ethical content. It was the eighth-century prophets who largely effected this ethicizing of holiness.[20] Although Jesus rarely used the words *holy* or *sanctified*,[21] it was he who gave full ethical content to the biblical idea of holiness.

Jesus is at once the disclosure of the God who is and of the man who is to be (Col. 1:15-29; 3:8-11; Eph. 4:11-16), "the new man, created in the likeness of God in true righteousness and holiness" (Eph. 4:24, literal rendering). Moreover, his death and resurrection defeated the powers of evil (Col. 2:13-15) and opened the fountain of sanctification for mankind (Eph. 5:25-27; Heb. 13:12; 1 John 1:7).

(3) The people God separates to himself, whom he cleanses from sin and defilement, he comes to indwell by the Holy Spirit (Eph. 2:11-22). This indwelling is both collective and individual (1 Cor. 3:15-16; 6:19-20). *It is this sanctifying indwelling of God the Holy Spirit that is New Testament sanctification.*[22] The Old Testament prophets foresaw this indwelling and predicted the gift of the Spirit as the mark of the messianic age (Ezek. 36:25-27; Joel 2:28-29; cf. Jer. 31:31-34). The New Testament apostles saw the Pentecostal outpouring of the Spirit as the sign that the eschaton ("the last days") had arrived (Acts 2:17; John 7:37-39 compared with Acts 2:33; Heb. 10:14-17). The Holy Spirit indwelling the Christian is therefore "the firstfruits" of his final redemption in Christ (Rom. 8:23), "the earnest of [his] inheritance" (Eph. 1:14; cf. 2 Cor. 1:21-22; Eph. 1:13-14), the foretaste of "the glory which shall be revealed" when Christ returns (Rom. 8:18; cf. 5:1-5). John the Baptist saw the baptism with the Holy Spirit as the crowning act of the Messiah for his people (Matt. 3:11-12; John 1:32-33), and the book of Acts makes the gift of the Spirit the *sine qua non* of New Testament Christianity (Acts 1:4-8; 2:1-4, 37-38; 8:14-17; 9:17; 10:44-45; 19:1-7). No wonder John the Revelator wrote, "The tabernacle of God is with men, and he will dwell with them" (Rev. 21:3).

3. Third, a dynamic theology of sanctification is *christological.* I have in mind what Gustaf Aulen calls the *Christus Victor* motif, or the dramatic view of the atonement.[23] While the New Testament views Christ's death and resurrection from many viewpoints—propitiation, expiation, redemption, ransom, reconciliation, et cetera—Aulen insists that the dominant motif is this *Christus Victor* idea, according to which Christ defeats the powers of evil and delivers man from the realm of darkness for life in the kingdom of God (see Col. 1:12-14; 2:8-23). By Jesus' death and resurrection, "God, who raised him from the dead . . . disarmed the principalities and powers and made a public example of them, triumphing over them in him" (Col. 2:12,

15, RSV). Because of the resurrection, the cross of Jesus was "the judgment of this world" in which "the ruler of this world [was] cast out" (John
12:31, RSV). The book of Hebrews declares, "Through death he destroyed
him who has the power of death, that is, the devil" (Heb. 2:14, freely translated). Moreover, his death was the death of the old Adam (potentially).[24] In
Jesus' flesh-and-blood body, God pronounced the doom of sin and routed
it from human personality "that the just requirement of the law might be
fulfilled in us, who walk not according to the flesh but according to the
Spirit" (Rom. 8:4, RSV). *Christus Victor* means Christ victorious for the new
humanity, which he bore in his flesh.[25] In order to grasp the full import of
this truth, we must remember that for Paul all men are ranged under either
Adam or Christ. By the disobedience of Adam, sin entered the world (Rom.
5:12).[26] As a consequence of his defection, we are born into a race that is in
revolt against God. But—

> *A second Adam to the fight*
>
> *And to the rescue came.*

By the obedience of the second Adam, the grace of God entered and re-
versed history: "For as through the one man's disobedience the many were
made sinners, even so through the obedience of the One the many will
be made righteous. And the Law came in that the transgression might in-
crease; but where sin increased, grace abounded all the more, that, as sin
reigned in death, even so grace might reign through righteousness to eternal
life through Jesus Christ our Lord" (Rom. 5:19-21, NASB).

Paul is thoroughly realist in his thinking here. The problem of evil is
indeed something that goes beyond questions of individual responsibility,
and salvation is more than a device for freeing an individual from his guilt:
it must cut at the root of corporate wrongness, which underlies individual
transgression. That is, according to Paul, what has actually been effected
by the work of Christ. In him, men are lifted into a new order in which
goodness is as powerful and dominant as was sin in the order represented
by Adam; or, rather, it is far more powerful and dominant.[27]

Paul's clear meaning here is that in Christ we may be recreated and that,
in this new creation, "the sin" that was introduced by Adam may be expelled! Romans 6 is the Magna Carta of Christian freedom from sin. In this
chapter we learn that this freedom "is no mere abstract theory or empty il-

lusion. The freedom for which Christ has set us free can be experienced and lived."[28] In Romans 7 and 8, we learn that this freedom is a kind of liberty that the law could never accomplish but which is experientially possible if we have faith in Christ.[29] Romans 5 through 8 is the *locus classicus* for Paul's teaching on sanctification. Everything he says in his other epistles on this topic finds its source in these chapters.

4. Furthermore, a dynamic theology of sanctification sees it preeminently *as the work of the Holy Spirit*. The grace of God is not only something without us, manifest in the passion and death of Christ and his victory over the hosts of evil, but also is "a power at work within us, directing its impact at the very citadel of our wills. This inward grace of God is God personally at work within us. It is God the Holy Ghost."[30]

It is God the Holy Spirit who enters the hidden recesses of the human spirit and works from within the subjectivity of man. From within our human person the Spirit awakens, vitalizes, renews, enlightens, purifies, strengthens, guides, and consecrates. C. W. Lowry describes the Spirit at work in us: "He is God in His special activity and agency of secret invasion and invisible occupation."[31] Lowry adds, "He is the *sanctifying* Spirit, making us holy [because] God is holy."[32] As George Croft Cell said, "Holiness is the third term of the Trinitarian revelation of God. This is the highest conceivable position for the doctrine of holiness in the Christian faith and interpretation."[33]

Understood this way, the sanctification of the Spirit is distinctively that purification of the heart from the remaining bias of sin and bringing it thereby into that devotement of love made perfect. It is this divine miracle of heart cleansing that is our distinctive witness.[34] We must be born of the Spirit, but we must also be baptized[35] with the Spirit. And to the inward work of sanctification the Holy Spirit bears gracious personal witness, thereby undercutting the need for any "sign" from God. It is this precious truth of entire sanctification by the Holy Spirit, which is our heritage as the sons of John and Charles Wesley.

Let us now return to the *Christus Victor* motif for the connecting link between redemption through Christ and sanctification by the Spirit. Romans 5—8, as I indicated, is the primary text for the Pauline doctrine of sanctification.[36] From this definitive passage, we learn that by union with the crucified-resurrected Christ we receive the life-giving, sanctifying Spirit.[37] Since Christ died for all, "therefore all have died" and live as he lives.[38]

The Spirit who raised Jesus from the dead can also give life to those in whom he dwells (Rom. 8:16-17). The Spirit who at the resurrection will "quicken [our] mortal bodies" now dwells in the believer as the sanctifying Spirit of Christ. If this indwelling is vital and real, the Christian's existence is "not in the flesh, but in the Spirit" (Rom. 8:9; cf. Gal. 5:25, RSV). That is to say, the indwelling Spirit is the believer's ethical sanctification (Rom. 8:2-9; Gal. 5:16-25). He is also the pledge of his final resurrection with Christ. The believer's life in the Spirit therefore embraces his existence in Christ from justification to glorification. This truth is the New Testament undergirding for a doctrine of progressive sanctification, which, as we shall see, includes three critical "moments": justification, entire sanctification, and glorification. The believer's sanctification begins in justification. In embracing the cross of Christ, he has "died to sin" (Rom. 6:1-2).[39] His old sin-dominated self ("the old man") has been "crucified" with Christ (Rom. 6:6; Gal. 5:24).[40] The Christian's death with Christ to sin is thus something that has already occurred, and Paul cites his baptism as proof of this fact.[41] Moreover, he has also been "raised up from the dead by the glory of the Father [to] walk in newness of life" (Rom. 6:4; 2 Cor. 5:17).[42] So Paul can say of both Christ and the believer, "For he who has died is freed [dedikaiotai] from sin" (Rom. 6:7, RSV).[43]

The walking in "newness of life" that the believer enjoys in Christ is also described as "new life of the Spirit" (7:6, RSV). It is also spoken of as walking "according to the Spirit [kata pneuma]" (8:4, RSV) and being "led by the Spirit" (v. 14). Although Paul does not use the term, this life in the Spirit is his doctrine of the new birth by the Spirit. As such, it is the beginning of both outward and inward sanctification.[44] By the same token, this initial sanctification is not entire sanctification. This fact is evident, not only from the fact that Christian believers are sometimes referred to as "yet carnal" (1 Cor. 3:1-4), and therefore possessing an imperfect faith (1 Thess. 3:10; 4:3-8; 5:23), but also from the fact that on the basis of their death and resurrection with Christ they are admonished (1) to "reckon" or "consider" themselves "to be dead indeed unto sin, but alive unto God through Jesus Christ our Lord" (Rom. 6:11),[45] and therefore (2) to "yield [themselves] to God as men who have been brought from death to life, and [their] members to God as instruments [or weapons] of righteousness" (v. 13, RSV).

We have now come to the "moment" of entire sanctification in Pauline thought. The critical aspect of this act is indicated by the use of the aorist tense in Romans 6:13 for the verb "yield." The believer is to bring the matter of his loyalty and servitude to a *moral crisis* in an act of unconditioned submission to the lordship of Christ.[46] When this submission happens, God's grace in Christ becomes completely regnant in his life, *expelling* sin from his heart.[47]

If the critical nature of Christian consecration is indicated by the employment of the aorist tense in Romans 6:13, the progressively unfolding nature of consecration is indicated by the use of the present tense in verse 16: "You know well enough that if you put yourselves at the disposal of a master, to obey him, you are slaves of the master whom you obey; and this is true whether you serve sin, with death as its result; or obedience, with righteousness as its result."[48] That is, the "yielded" life is a life put at God's disposal "moment by moment," as Wesley insisted.[49] This way of living is what Wesley, after Jesus, calls "abiding in Christ,"[50] and what Paul means by "walk[ing] by the Spirit" (Gal. 5:16, RSV; see Gal. 5:16-25, RSV, and Rom. 8:5-9, RSV).

In 7:1-6 Paul uses the metaphor of marriage to enforce the truth that dying and rising with Christ means belonging to him as one who has been called to a new life of righteousness in the Holy Spirit. The Christian has not only died to sin, he has also died to the law. No longer under the binding power of the law, he is "free." But he is *not* free "for any and all alliances. He is free for one only. He has been given freedom for a specific reason: 'In order that [he] might belong to another.' That 'other' is Christ 'who has been raised from the dead.'"[51]

This metaphor proves fascinating to Paul, and he draws two amazing conclusions from it. (1) Under the law God's people were married to the flesh, and the issue of that union was "fruit unto death," or "the motions of sins" (Rom. 7:5; explained in 7:7-25; cf. Gal. 5:22-25). (2) But the new marriage also has its issue, "fruit unto God," which Paul defines as service "in the new life of the Spirit" (Rom. 7:4; v. 6, RSV; explained in 8:1-17).

But to be dead to the law is more than something that happened at conversion; it must be translated into a life "in the Spirit."[52]

The progressively unfolding nature of this life in the Spirit is beautifully stated in Second Corinthians: "And we all, with unveiled face, beholding the glory of the Lord, are being changed into his likeness from one degree of glory to another; for this comes from the Lord who is the Spirit" (3:18, RSV).[53] This passage describes the lifelong growth in Christlikeness, which will only be consummated when we see Christ. At that moment of glorification, "we shall be like him; for we shall see him as he is" (1 John 3:2; cf. Phil. 3:20-21).

The life of holiness, however, is lived only in the body of Christ, understood as the divinely created *koinonia* of the Spirit. This body is not "mystical." It is both "invisible" and "visible," composed according to the New Testament, of all baptized believers in Christ.[54] To be "in Christ" and therefore "in the Spirit" is no individualistic psychological experience; it is to be incorporated into Christ's living body, into the fellowship of the saints (1 Cor. 12:12-27; Eph. 4:1-16).[55] New Testament holiness is therefore social as well as personal.[56] So the new man in Christ is "no 'Lone Ranger' who rides off in lonely individualism to serve God and become righteous [but is] one who grows into his Christian life in continual relationship with others who, like him, are living in Christ's presence, without whose mutual guidance, witness, reproof and sometimes discipline no holy life is possible."[57]

5. Finally, a dynamic biblical theology of sanctification is *eschatological*: sanctification by the Spirit occurs "between the times."[58] As Peter pointed out in his Pentecostal sermon, the sanctifying gift of the Spirit is the crowning work of God in these "last days," which stretch between Pentecost and the Parousia (Acts 2:17-21). In Christ we have freedom from sin through the gift of the indwelling, sanctifying Spirit of God. God's new order is a kingdom of grace in which sin may be expelled from the human heart. But Paul insists, "We have this treasure in earthen vessels" (2 Cor. 4:7). This splendid work of God—this transformation of our lives into the image of Christ by the Spirit (2 Cor. 3:18)—occurs in physical bodies, which have not yet been fully redeemed (Rom. 8:23-24). Our salvation may be full, but it is not yet final.[59]

In Romans 8:17-28, Paul writes about "this present time" between the ages, a time of suffering, bafflement, imperfection, infirmity—a time of "travail" that betokens the birth of a new world of perfect liberty and eternal life. F. Godet has caught the significance of this perspective for a doctrine of sanctification. He writes, "As to the spirit we are in the age to come; as to the body, in the present age."[60] Although the body of the fully sanctified is no longer an instrument of sin (Rom. 6:13, 19), it is still essentially unredeemed.

As men and women indwelt by the Spirit, we are still beset with "infirmities" that cause us to "groan" within ourselves "with sighs too deep for words." These weaknesses encompass the whole array of human frailties: the racial effects of sin in our bodies and minds, the scars of past sinful living, our prejudices that hinder God's purposes, our neuroses that bring emotional depressions and cause us at times to "act out of character," our temperamental idiosyncrasies, our human weaknesses and fretfulness, our frailties that make us fail God at times in spite of ourselves, and a thousand faults our mortal flesh is heir to. It is these weaknesses that cause our "involuntary transgressions"[61] of God's perfect law and that cause us inevitably to fall short of the perfect law of love.[62] A full-orbed doctrine of Christian perfection must therefore place the truth of entire sanctification within the framework of "this present time" in which the two ages overlap, a period marked by the "infirmities" of the flesh. The tyranny of the flesh is ended by the sanctifying presence of the Holy Spirit (Rom. 8:8-9), but not the weakness of the flesh.[63] In Philippians Paul puts this truth in fullest perspective. First, "It is God who is at work in [me], both to will and to work for His good pleasure" (Phil. 2:13, NASB). But in view of the fact that the resurrection is yet future, I have not yet been perfected (3:12),[64] even though I may be "perfect" (v. 15) in the sense that I am now "in tune with my redeemed destiny in Christ."[65] Nevertheless, "I am confident of this very thing, that He who began a good work in [me] will perfect it until the day of Christ Jesus" (1:6, NASB).

For this reason, Paul says in Romans, "In this hope we were saved" (8:24, RSV), the hope of the glory that will be revealed when Christ returns. "If Christianity be not altogether restless eschatology," says Karl Barth, "there remains in it no relationship whatever to Christ."[66] But we can rejoice with

Paul: "But now Christ has been raised from the dead, the first fruits of those who are asleep. For since by man came death, by a man also came the resurrection of the dead. For as in Adam all die, so also in Christ shall all be made alive. But each in his own order: Christ the first fruits, after that those who are Christ's at His coming" (1 Cor. 15:20-23, NASB). To whom be glory forever. Amen.

IX
THE SIGNIFICANCE
OF WATER BAPTISM

—⚬⚬⚬—

The Church of the Nazarene from its earliest days emphasized personal reli-
gious experience. This emphasis posed a danger that the classical sacraments
of the church would receive minimal emphasis and thus not be observed. Dr.
Greathouse, in his concern that the church not be sectarian in its practices, or
lack thereof, wrote this document, published in tract form for the Department of
Evangelism. He was himself baptized as an infant and never felt any necessity of
being rebaptized. Child baptism was at that time a more controversial topic than
it apparently is at the present time; hence the rite of dedication is acknowledged.
This tract emphasized the importance, even necessity, of baptism without being
sectarian with regard to its mode.

CHRIST COMMANDS his church to disciple all nations and baptize
those who believe (Matt. 28:19; Mark 16:15-16). To omit baptizing Christ's
disciples is to reject his clear command and to set our wisdom above his.
The *Manual* of the Church of the Nazarene states, "Christian baptism is . . .
to be administered to believers."

The words of Paul in 1 Corinthians 1:13-17 are not a belittlement of
baptism but a protest against the mistaken notion of certain Corinthians
who supposed they had been baptized into the name of the one who had administered the rite to them rather than into the undivided name of Christ.

Baptism, the Symbol of Entry into the Church
From the day of Pentecost, baptism has been the symbolic rite of entry
into the Christian community (see Acts 2:38, 41; 8:12; 10:47-48). In New

Testament times, the new convert would confess "Jesus is Lord"[1] and be baptized into the community of salvation (Rom. 10:8-10; cf. Matt. 16:15-18; 1 Cor. 12:3; 1 John 4:15). Later this simple confession was expanded into the Apostles' Creed, which is still used in this way. In our communion, reception into the Church of the Nazarene follows this rite of entrance into the visible body of Christ.

As the ancient Israelites "were baptized into Moses" in the Red Sea (1 Cor. 10:2, so by water we are "baptized into Christ Jesus" (Rom. 6:3). In both cases baptism means initiation into a community, which is being saved by a divine deliverer—ancient Israel by God's saving activity through Moses, the Christian church by God's saving activity through Jesus Christ.

The New Testament church simply did not include any unbaptized Christians, except those who were being prepared for baptism. True, we are incorporated into the living body of Christ by the Spirit, but in the New Testament this was followed immediately by Christian baptism, which incorporated these persons into the visible body of Christ. First Corinthians 12:12-13 is a passage that indicates this dual incorporation.

The Significance of Christian Baptism

Christian baptism ritually symbolizes the miracle of God's saving grace.

1. It pictures the washing away of our sins, the bath of regeneration (Acts 22:16; Titus 3:5; 1 Pet. 3:21).

2. It dramatizes our death, burial, and resurrection with Christ (Rom. 6:1-4; Col. 2:9-13). As the New Testament believer went down into the waters of baptism, he "died" to his old life; as he came forth from the water he arose to "walk in newness of life." This is still the dramatic symbol of baptism in non-Christian lands. Baptism cuts the new man off from his old life and marks him henceforth as Christ's man. When it is so understood, baptism is a powerful deterrent to backsliding. Baptism puts our death to sin into the arena of public fact. As Jesus' burial was proof of his death to sin, Christian baptism is intended to demonstrate our death to sin. As such, it incorporates us into the full benefits of Christ's atonement and becomes our pledge to holiness.

3. It portrays our "put[ting] on Christ" (Gal. 3:26-29; Rom. 13:14; Col. 3:9-11). In the early church, the person about to be baptized laid aside his

old garments (which symbolized his old manner of life) as he stepped into the water; as he emerged, he was given new white clothes (which pictured the new robe of Christ's righteousness and holiness, which was his). Thus, he "put on the new man," or Christ, in a dramatic ceremony that told the world the old had passed and the new had come. This practice is behind that of our putting on new clothes at Easter, since in later centuries Easter became the time when many were baptized.

4. It symbolizes the baptism with the Holy Spirit (Matt. 3:11; Acts 1:4-5). The Pentecostal gift of the Holy Spirit is associated with Christian baptism throughout the New Testament, but especially in Acts. Sometimes this gift seems to come at the time of baptism (Acts 9:17-18; 19:4-6); again, it was separated by some length of time (8:12-17); yet again, sometimes the baptism with the Holy Spirit preceded water baptism (10:44-48). Nevertheless, the reality symbolized by water baptism is not experienced until we have been filled with the Spirit and cleansed from sin. Water baptism is a pledge and seal of Spirit baptism.

The Mode of Baptism

In the New Testament baptism seems to have been either by immersion or by effusion (or pouring). Luke 11:38, which says literally that Jesus did not "baptize" himself before dinner according to pharisaic ritual, is proof that the Greek verb *baptizo* did not mean simply "to immerse or dip." It seems that Romans 6:1-4 and Colossians 2:9-13 most naturally suggest immersion. However, other passages seem to indicate pouring. "Having stood up" (literally) Paul was baptized in his room in the house on Straight Street in Damascus (Acts 9:17-18). The Philippian jailer and his household were baptized in the middle of the night in their apartment at the jail (16:32-34). Simon Peter commanded water to be *brought in* to baptize Cornelius and his household in the room where they had just been baptized with the Holy Spirit (10:47-48).

In the first manual of the Christian church, called *The Teaching of the Twelve Apostles* (ca. AD 135), we have the earliest reference to the mode of baptism. It instructs:

Having first recited all these things [the Creed], baptize "in the name of the Father and of the Son and the Holy Spirit" in living [running] water but if thou hast not living water, then baptize in other water; and if thou art not able in cold, then in warm. But if thou hast neither, then pour water on the head thrice in the name of the Father and of the Son and of the Holy Spirit.

Our Nazarene practice of administering baptism "by sprinkling, pouring, or immersion, according to the choice of the applicant" (Article XIII) thus appears to be in line with the practice of the early church.

Child Baptism

Our article on baptism also permits Christian parents or guardians to present "young children" for Christian baptism. Many believe infant baptism is indicated by the cases of "household baptism" mentioned in the New Testament (Acts 16:15, 33; 18:8; 1 Cor. 1:16, etc.). In the use of the term "household," young children were specifically included at that time. Paul seems to indicate that baptism is the equivalent of Jewish circumcision, which was administered to infants (see Acts 21:21; Col. 2:11-12). As such, baptism is "the sacrament of prevenient grace," an outward symbol of the grace that God will exercise through the lives of parents who thereby pledge to give the child necessary Christian training.

Many Christian leaders, however, believe it is preferable to dedicate infants publicly and to reserve Christian baptism for that moment when the child understands the meaning of the rite and is able to appropriate for himself the rich benefits of the sacred ceremony.

"Go therefore and make disciples of all nations, baptizing them in the name of the Father and of the Son and of the Holy Spirit, teaching them to observe all that I have commanded you; and lo, I am with you always, to the close of the age" (Matt. 28:19-20).

X
MY VISION FOR NAZARENE WORSHIP

This presentation was given during a chapel service at Nazarene Theological Seminary in 1989 and subsequently published in The Preacher's *Magazine, December/ January/February 1989-90. It was originally titled "The Present Crisis in Nazarene Worship." We have edited the title and minimal content to more nearly fit the purpose of this collection. Among the other emphases of this lecture, it reflects Dr. Greathouse's recognition that a people's theology is profoundly influenced by their music. His awareness of the relationship of theology and music is the basis for his insistence on the importance of the use of hymns in public worship.*

FOR MY ENTIRE MINISTRY, from my first home mission pastorate to the present hour, it has been my deep concern that Nazarenes learn better how to worship. I am persuaded that nothing we do as Christ's ministers is more important than our own personal worship and our conduct of public worship, in which we have the high privilege of leading God's people into a living encounter with him in his holiness and his grace.

My personal history will perhaps explain my acknowledged bias. I was born, baptized, and nourished in Methodism. My earliest memories are of kneeling with my parents to receive Holy Communion and of singing with the congregation the great hymns of the church, which celebrate his majesty, glory, and saving mercy. The worship of Almighty God was a powerful molding influence upon my mind and heart long before I was aware of what was happening. For all this, I praise God.

It was through the Church of the Nazarene, however, that I encountered Christ as my personal Savior as a high school junior in a home mission tent campaign. Three years later, after my freshman year at Bethany Peniel College, I found myself the supply pastor of a struggling little flock in Jackson, Tennessee. I completed my final three years of undergraduate study at the Methodist college in that town. In chapel there, as at Vanderbilt Divinity School for five additional years (still as a Nazarene pastor), my understanding of worship and my appreciation for the church's hymnody was deepened. At the same time, I felt entirely comfortable in revival and camp meeting services where spiritual demonstration, weeping, shouting, and sometimes even "sanctified dancing" were the order of the day. Then, as now, I found a deep response to Dr. Bresee's call: "Oh, Nazarenes, keep the glory down"—along with an abhorrence of trumped up emotionalism. With Dr. J. B. Chapman, I say, "I was born in the fire, and I cannot settle for the smoke."

I yearn for only one thing: the manifest presence of God in the midst of his people, whether in the earthquake and fire or in the voice of gentle stillness. True worship, I am convinced, is the eternal spark of heavenly flame that inspires, refines, sustains, and builds up the life of the church. Worship is the highest act of which a creature of God is capable, for the "chief end of man is to *glorify God and enjoy him forever.*"

For me, the most comprehensive and satisfying definition of worship is that of Archbishop William Temple who wrote,

Worship is the quickening of the conscience by the holiness of God; it is the nourishment of the mind by the truth of God; it is the purifying of our imagination by the beauty of God; it is the opening of the heart to the love of God; it is the surrender of the will to the purpose of God—and all of this gathered up in adoration, the most selfless emotion of which human nature is capable and therefore the chief remedy for that self-centeredness which is our original sin.[1]

Such worship can take place in either Westminster Cathedral or the humblest Nazarene chapel if the people of God there assembled have met to ascribe to him "worth-ship"—to give to him alone the worth, the value, the honor, the glory, the adoration, which are his due as our Creator, Sustainer, and Redeemer—and to join intelligently and feelingly with the angelic beings in singing, "Worthy is the Lamb that was slain to receive power, and riches, and wisdom, and strength, and honour, and glory, and blessing" (Rev. 5:12).

It is against this background of conviction and understanding that I must attempt to assess the present status of Nazarene worship. My task is made extremely difficult, however, not only by my own limited observation of what is actually going on throughout our movement in this matter of worship, but also by the fact that I recognize there are many different models of worship style among us, even in the same city. We must allow for variations in forms and styles of worship, to recognize the widely differing cultural needs in any given community; however—and this part is the most important one—there are certainly some norms by which we can evaluate whether or not true worship is taking place where we are or under our ministry.

For a starter, let me suggest that in many churches confusion exists as to what really constitutes worship. Many pastors apparently do not know how to plan a service of worship. They regularly ignore the elements that must go into true worship, which permits their services to fall into an informal formality that stifles the Holy Spirit. Of course, this situation is nothing new. More than forty years ago, General Superintendent Chapman complained that many Nazarene services had more of the atmosphere of "an old-fashioned mountain corn-husking" than of the worship of almighty God. He was struck by the fact that many pastors did not know the difference between hymns (which are addressed to God—or at least are God-centered in content) and gospel songs (which are subjective and experience-centered). The latter may be appropriate, he said, as the service moves into a more intimate and personal mood, but a service of worship should open—as does the Lord's Prayer—with the acknowledgment and adoration of God, with hymns like "Come, Thou Almighty King" or "O for a Thousand Tongues," music and words that enable the soul to rise into God's presence. He was also bothered that the Scripture reading was often limited to the quoting of the text for the sermon—a deplorable practice—and that a special song was often inserted before the sermon, simply to have a special, when a hymn such as "Break Thou the Bread of Life" would be far more appropriate.

In many sections of the church, this lack of understanding about authentic worship remains a problem. More times than I wish to admit, I have had to remind the minister of music or the pastor, who was opening the morning worship in the district assembly, that "Victory in Jesus" was not quite appropriate at that moment. Unless a service of true worship was planned, for the past two years I've had a standard suggestion, that the morning assembly open with "Come, Thou Fount of ev'ry blessing; / Tune my heart to sing Thy grace! / Streams of mercy, never ceasing! / Call for songs of loudest praise." When the service of worship was to be deferred until the eleven o'clock hour, I still insisted that the assembly open with a hymn such as "I Love Thy kingdom, Lord! / The house of Thine abode! / The Church our blest Redeemer bought, / With His own precious blood."

Not many months ago, I was in one of our larger churches in the Midwest, a truly great and influential church. I was disappointed and grieved in spirit not to be able to join in singing a single hymn of worship that morning. It was a gospel-song service throughout. Although the people sang lustily, I sensed little of the "wonder, love, and praise" my heart yearned to experience. The entire service was experience-centered, and when I stood to preach, I had to generate my own worship. My soul felt cheated that morning. The pastor and minister of music are spiritually minded and experienced men of God, but apparently, neither has been taught the difference between "hymns, songs, and spiritual songs" or what constitutes an authentic service of worship. (Incidentally, I still see a valid distinction between the morning worship service and an evening gospel service where informality and songs of testimony are quite appropriate.)

I find myself in reluctant agreement with John R. Stott's critique:

We evangelicals do not know much about worship. Evangelism is our specialty, not worship. We have little sense of the greatness of almighty God . . . Our worship services are often ill prepared, slovenly, mechanical, perfunctory, and dull . . . Much of public worship is ritual without reality, form without power, religion without God.[2]

Contrast Stott's assessment with Dr. Bresee's description of morning worship in the old Glory Barn of Los Angeles First Church:

It was the fire within that gilded the boards with glory and made them shimmer and shine with the light of heaven. When the multitude has gathered, and there are hundreds of one mind and heart, and the Holy Ghost descends in his plentitude and power, that place is garnished with a beauty and glory in comparison with which all the adorning of Solomon's Temple would be barrenness. Every board shines with the jeweled beauty of the New Jerusalem. What are carved marble and overlaying of gold and trimmings of silver; what are arches and turrets and spires, in comparison with the beauty of the Lord and the glory of the Divine Presence?[3]

Ideal perhaps, but a worthy ideal for every Nazarene pastor and congregation. Those who come into our services should be able to say, "This is indeed the house of God, the very gate of heaven."

A second critical area is the growing tendency to crowd out congregational singing with special music. If the church is not large enough to have a trained choir, they can at least assemble a gospel quartet, or a gospel combo! This past October I had the high privilege of a seventeen-day preaching mission in Great Britain. What made the visit such a great spiritual benefit to me was the opportunity I enjoyed in each service—but one—of singing with the people of England, Scotland, and Ireland, not only many of John and Charles Wesley's hymns (sung to tunes I'd never heard but soon learned to love), but also those of other great hymnists such as John Newton, Horatio Bonar, and Isaac Watts, men who knew how to describe in poetic language the soul's aspirations for and praise of our great Redeemer.

I said, in every service but one. I must be careful and considerate of what I say here because that particular Irish church was alive and growing. But since apparently it was the first time a general superintendent had visited them, they prepared almost an hour of special music—for the Lord, I'm sure—but also for me and for the lord mayor of that city and his lady who would come that evening. The service opened with the heartfelt singing of Charles Wesley's "O for a Thousand Tongues," but that hymn was the end of the congregational singing that evening. For about an hour, the youth choir, the ladies' ensemble, the men's choir, and the combined choirs sang and sang and sang. When I was presented to preach, it was already past nine o'clock, and I felt I was speaking into a spiritual vacuum. The sermon God had used in other services to expand my own soul and lift God's people, that night was a laborious struggle. What was wrong? An hour-long stream of "specials" had dissipated the spirit of worship. The lord mayor's wife commented to me kindly after the service, "I wish they had furnished us the words to their songs so I could have followed along." Her felt need, apparently like mine, was to participate in the worship.

Robert E. Webber has rightly said, "*Worship* is a verb."[4] It is not what the people passively listen to that constitutes worship; it is what they do. In overemphasizing special numbers to the neglect of congregational singing, we are robbing God's people of one of the best ways to involve them in worship, provided the hymns and songs are prayerfully chosen. I would add a second proviso: the pastors should model for their people the worship of God by their own spirit and participation.

Closely related to the growing practice of substituting special music for congregational singing is the drift toward religious entertainment in our services. This place is not the one to go into all the reasons for such a drift. I will simply state it bluntly: This practice represents an invasion of the church by the spirit of this age. A narcissistic culture demands entertainment, and we can be religiously entertained and left untouched by the Spirit of Christ. In another context, Dean Inge once warned, "When the church marries the spirit of the age, she will be left a widow in the next generation."[5] This outcome is what has been referred to as the danger of "the secularization of our people's perceptions." Moreover, without the intention of unholy alliance, the church is suddenly in a vulnerable position.

I agree with James Spruce who writes, "The tension for the church is to remain a reliable witness by refusing to sacrifice its credibility to the god of worldly popularity . . . And it is within the sacred precincts of the church at worship that we are most severely tested."[6] Spruce continues, "One of the obvious testing grounds is Christian music, where the blending of sacred and secular music is so subtly done, that the difference between Christian praise and worldly entertainment is often confused if not indistinguishable. The response of the passive worshiper is often failure to distinguish between what is truly entertaining and what is truly God-honoring."[7]

The situation I have described is not much of an issue for people at a Saturday night "praise gathering" or at a downtown concert hall. But what about Sunday morning, when we gather in church to worship? Are we then also being entertained by the musicians or the preacher? Are we more impressed with the performer, showmanship, and decibels than we are with the message and words? The current practice of applauding at least leaves the impression that the skill of a performer has drawn the response, rather than the message of truth being conveyed. This new practice of applauding is most disturbing to me when the singer has obviously been under the anointing of the Spirit, and my soul, hushed in wonder and adoration, is assaulted by loud applause!

If the people are only passive observers or spectators, their chances of confusing the medium with the message are very high. Worship is not something done before or for the congregation, as if those leading the service are the actors and the congregation the audience. No, but as Søren Kierkegaard reminds us, the worship leaders are simply "prompters" for the true "actors," who are the people of God gathered to ascribe worth, honor, and praise to almighty God. The "performance" is not by the leaders but by the congregation. George Frederic Handel's classic statement in 1741 after the premier of his *Messiah* is still valid: "Sir, I should be sorry if I only entertained them. I had hoped it would make them better." Being made better, says Spruce, has little or nothing to do with whether or not we have a sense of fulfillment through being emotionally entertained. He continues,

But it has everything to do with a sense of fulfillment through servanthood. The sad consequence of passivity is the loss of servanthood for the fun of being a spectator. And in an age of Christian idols, fans find it easy to follow the stars. When our favorites are performing either on television or at an all-night sing or are moving from church to church, who has time for servanthood? Who has time to visit the nursing home? Who provides a meal for the poor?[8]

Those observations are not intended as a criticism of Christian artists who sing or preach for us. They too have a duty to fulfill before God. They have the responsibility and privilege of helping us to praise God too; however, let us place the Christian response to human need where it really belongs. It belongs, Spruce concludes, "On the shoulders of the people who come to enjoy good feelings or their old-time religion but are rarely, if ever, moved to faithful servanthood."[9]

Theologically, this means that religious entertainment, in harmony with the spirit of this age, tends to reinforce the egocentricity of our fallen humanity. Whereas, true worship, as William Temple believes, moves us to the surrender of our wills to the purpose of God: "in adoration, the most selfless emotion of which human nature is capable, provides the remedy for that self-centeredness which is our original sin." To me, this is the heart of the present crisis in Nazarene worship.

Underlying this crisis is a cultural shift in the way people think and feel. Robert Webber has put it well:

> There was a time when the idea of mystery was more a part of our thinking than now. God was in His heavens high, holy, and lifted up. In worship there was a sense of awe and reverence in the presence of the one who was wholly other. But now we have . . . so reduced [God] to clichés and formulas that the mystery has disappeared. Our approach to God is intellectual and scientific in one extreme and excessively "buddy-buddy" on the other; both are sorely lacking in imagination.[10]

We holiness evangelicals have not escaped this secularization of life and the influence of our narcissistic culture. We rejoice in our "Body Life," as we should, but our worship tends, in some churches, to be too much a reflection of our experience in Christ. Great hymns like "Holy, Holy, Holy" and "O God, Our Help in Ages Past" lose the depth of their meaning in human-centered worship; then our services tend to become exercises in showmanship and decibels. The celebration of our oneness in Christ is precious, but it must not be divorced from the sense of God's sublime glory and matchless grace, which move true worshipers to be "lost in wonder, love, and praise."

Despite the scientific, secularized, human-centered thinking of this present age, God is still God. He remains indeed "the high and holy One who inhabits eternity." He has not abdicated his throne, and he is worthy of our praise as our Creator and our Redeemer in Christ. With that truth in mind, we must find ways to instill a sense of awe within worshipers. We must help them to understand why they are in church on Sunday and what it means to bow down before the infinite God in that mixture of awe, wonder, and joy, which we call "worship"!

As Christ's ministers, we must "take time to be holy" by living in the Word and sustaining a deep personal relationship with God in Christ. From that connection should flow a spirit of awe, praise, and adoration that will communicate itself to the worshipers who gather in our churches on the Lord's Day. "We must commit ourselves to the biblical view of knowing that God deserves so much more than He is getting from us," Spruce reminds us.[11] Of course, in our frailty, we will never give God all the glory he deserves, but we can give him our best! And our best means that God paid a great price for us to be able to sing, "Worthy is the Lamb that was slain" (Rev. 5:12).

XI

HOLINESS: WHY ALL
THE CONFUSION?

This article was written subsequent to Dr. Greathouse's retirement as general superintendent. It appeared in the March 1996 issue of the denominational periodical Herald of Holiness *(now* Holiness Today*). The title and opening passage reflect the situation near the end of the twentieth century when the church was experiencing an identity crisis regarding its distinguishing tenet of entire sanctification. The author remains fully committed to the doctrine to which his entire career was committed. He is still convinced that John Wesley's teaching, which he believes is true to Scripture, is the path through that crisis.*

"HAVE YOU been sanctified?" the pastor asked the counselee. "Oh please, Pastor, don't bring that up," she protested. "I have enough problems as it is." Holiness, a problem? Unfortunately, for some, it *is*.

Why the confusion? It should not arise from the doctrine as derived from Scripture. The truth is simple. Holiness is God's provision *for* us by Christ (1 Cor. 1:30; Rom. 8:1-4; Heb. 10:11-18) and his work *within* us by the Holy Spirit (Ezek. 36:27; 2 Thess. 2:13; Rom. 8:3, 9, 13), freeing us from sin (from its power in the new birth [Rom. 6:1-7, 17-18; 7:4-6], its corruption in entire sanctification [2 Cor. 7:1; 1 Thess. 4:8; 5:23-24]) and progressively restoring us in Christlikeness in spirit, attitude, and lifestyle (2 Cor. 3:18).

Experientially, the Holy Spirit is "the immediate cause of all holiness in us."[1] He applies to our hearts the benefits of Christ's redemptive sufferings: "He is God in His special activity and agency of secret invasion and invisible occupation."[2] He is thus the *sanctifying* Spirit, making us partakers of the divine holiness (2 Pet. 1:4; Heb. 12:10).

Holiness is the work and gift of the triune God. The Father wills and plans our holiness; the Son reveals and provides holiness; the Spirit imparts holiness, *God's* holiness. As Harriet Auber puts it,

> And every virtue we possess,
>
> And every victory won,
>
> And every thought of holiness
>
> Are His alone.

Let us briefly trace the development of holiness in personal experience.

1. Holiness has its roots in prevenient grace, in unresisted conviction. In the unconverted state, it originates with "the sanctifying work of the Spirit" who constrains and enables us to "obey Jesus Christ and be sprinkled with His blood" (1 Pet. 1:2, NASB).

2. Holiness of *life* begins in conversion, "by the washing of regeneration and renewal in the Holy Spirit" (Titus 3:5, RSV). This experience is the beginning of both outward and inward holiness (see 1 Cor. 6:9-11). The life the Spirit imparts is a *holy* life. Therefore, as new creatures in Christ, we begin to "walk in the same manner as He walked" (1 John 2:6, NASB; see 2 Cor. 5:17; 1 John 2:1-6). A new pattern of obedience has displaced in us the old pattern of sinning and disobedience (see 1 John 3:3-10; 5:18). *One* standard is required of *all*: "As obedient children, do not be conformed to the former lusts which were yours in your ignorance, but like the Holy One who called you, be holy yourselves also in all your behavior" (1 Pet. 1:14-15, NASB).

3. Holiness of *heart* results from the deeper purging of entire sanctification. "Purity of heart," says Kierkegaard, "is to will one thing." Heart holiness is the perfection of the purity that begins in regeneration: "Therefore, having these promises, beloved, let us cleanse ourselves from all defilement of flesh and spirit, perfecting holiness in the fear of God" (2 Cor. 7:1, NASB).

John Wesley spoke of this perfected holiness as entire sanctification or Christian perfection.[3] Taking into account more fully the Old Testament "promise of the Father," the holiness movement also refers to it as the purifying baptism with the Holy Spirit (see Ezek. 36:25-27; Jer. 31:31-34; Mal. 3:2-8; Matt. 3:11-12; Luke 3:16-17; Acts 1:4-5; 2:1-36 [cf. v. 33 with John 7:39]).

"Entire sanctification," Wesley explains, is neither more nor less than pure love—"love excluding sin; love filling the heart, taking up the whole capacity of the soul. . . . How strongly [does this] imply the being saved from all sin! For as long as love takes up the whole heart, what room is there for sin therein?"[4]

He continues, "This love that fulfills the law is the essence of Christian perfection" (see Rom. 13:8-10; 1 Tim. 1:5). It is blamelessness rather than faultlessness (see Eph. 1:3-4; Col. 1:22-23). He further explains, "Pure love reigning alone in the heart and life—this is the whole of scriptural perfection."[5] Wesley, however, makes an important qualification: "But even that love increases more and more, till we 'grow up in all things into Him that is our Head'; till we attain 'the measure of the stature of the fulness of Christ.'"[6]

4. Perfected Christlikeness is the final manifestation of holiness; this grace awaits the resurrection (see Phil. 3:10-15, 20-21; Rom. 8:18-25; 1 John 3:2). Meanwhile, in E. Stanley Jones's fine phrase, we are but "Christians in the making." Nevertheless, we are "confident of this very thing, that He who began a good work in you will perfect it until the day of Christ Jesus" (Phil. 1:6, NASB).

There we have in bold outline Christian holiness as understood by those of us who call ourselves the heirs of John Wesley and Paul.

Why, then, all the confusion about holiness? Answer: It arises from a failure to hold to these scriptural guidelines. Certain unscriptural ideas have developed in the "folk theology" of the church, such as the following:

1. The tendency to think of sin as a "thing" that, once eradicated, is gone forever. Rather, in Scripture, sin is a disease; holiness is moral and spiritual health restored. To remain spiritually whole, we must observe the laws of spiritual health.[7] Again, sin is darkness; holiness is light. Spiritual darkness returns when we fail to walk in the light (see 1 John 1:4-7).

2. The tendency to think of entire sanctification as the *end*, rather than the means to spiritual maturity. It is the end only of sin—our corrupt self-centeredness, our self-sovereignty, our imagined self-sufficiency. Once this conflict is resolved, we can begin to grow in true Christlikeness.

3. The tendency to think of heart holiness as the eradication of our human drives and instincts. While these urges are essential to our humanity, they must be kept subservient to the will of God—in the power of the Spirit (Rom. 8:13; 1 Cor. 9:27). Sin may once again reign in our mortal bodies if we yield to these desires (Rom. 6:12-13). They are not, however, sinful *per se*. Temptation does not become sin until it gains the consent of our will (James 1:14-15).

4. The tendency to think of Christian perfection as a state of sinlessness. Those filled with God's pure love are still finite, human, and fallible. Inevitably, they fall short of God's perfect law of love and are guilty of "involuntary transgressions." The holiest of persons, therefore, need to pray, "Forgive us our debts, as we forgive our debtors." They still need the blood to atone for their "coming short of the full mind that was in Christ, and walking less accurately than they might have done after their Divine Pattern."[8]

5. The tendency to forget that our holiness is always a *derived* holiness, mediated to us and maintained only as Christ lives in us and we in him. I conclude with my favorite quote from Wesley:

> The holiest of men still need Christ, as their Prophet, as "the light of the world." For he does not give them light, but from moment to moment; the instant he withdraws, all is darkness. They still need Christ as their King; for God does not give them a stock of holiness. But unless they receive a supply every moment, nothing but unholiness would remain. They still need "Christ as their Priest, to make atonement for their holy things. Even perfect holiness is acceptable to God only through Jesus Christ."[9]

XII
THE SECRET OF HOLY LIVING

This article was published in the Herald of Holiness *in June 1997 and in Illustrated Bible Life in the December—February 1996-97 issue. It reflects not only his lifelong emphasis on the enabling power of the Holy Spirit, which became such a central focus of his own experience, but also his appropriation of both John Wesley and Scripture.*

"I'LL NEVER make it!" she moaned. "The harder I try to live for God, the more miserably I fail. I read my Bible and pray, I go to church faithfully. I tithe. I try to witness to my neighbors. But every day I fail God. I'll never make it!"

When her pastor smiled, she broke into tears. "Please don't make fun of me," she protested; "this is no joke." "I know it's no joke," he said, "but I thank God you found it out. *You can't make it*—but *Christ has already made it for you.*"

Christ has already won the victory over sin and all the hosts of darkness arrayed against us. As the apostle John assures, "You are of God, little children, *and have overcome them,* because He who is in you is greater than he who is in the world" (1 John 4:4, NKJV, emphasis added).

Paul puts it this way: "Christ Jesus . . . has become for us . . . righteousness, holiness and redemption" (1 Cor. 1:30, NIV). Christ is our holiness as well as our righteousness. Dying for us, he is our righteousness; living and reigning, he is our holiness.

"Called unto holiness," praise His dear name!
This blessed secret to faith now made plain:
Not our own righteousness, but Christ within,
Living, and reigning, and saving from sin.

—Lelia N. Morris

The following three truths are foundational to holy living:

A Distinction to Be Grasped

We must keep in the forefront of our thinking the distinction between the law and the gospel. Otherwise, we consign ourselves to confusion and unnecessary condemnation. We say with Martin Luther that the law is what God *requires* of us; the gospel is what, on the basis of his promises, he *gives* to us. The old covenant was indeed a covenant of grace, but its central element was law. Asked which was the Great Commandment of the law, Jesus answered: "'You shall love the Lord your God with all your heart . . . You shall love your neighbor as yourself.' On these two commandments hang all the law and the prophets" (Matt. 22:37, 39-40, NRSV).

The weakness of the old covenant was that it contained no offer of the life-giving, sanctifying Spirit. The distinctive nature of the new covenant is precisely the promise of the Spirit. Through his Son, "God has done what the law, weakened by the flesh, could not do" (Rom. 8:3, NRSV). Through Christ, God has vanquished sin and opened the floodgates of the sanctifying Spirit (see vv. 1-4).

The law remains the divine requirement, deepened and refined by Jesus; but the good news is that the Spirit who fulfills the law has been given! If the central feature of the old covenant is law (what God commands), the heart of the new is the gospel (what God gives according to his promise).

A Promise to Be Appropriated

Writing to the Galatians, who were being seduced by Jewish legalists to return to the law, Paul penned, "You foolish Galatians! Who has bewitched you? Before your very eyes Jesus Christ was clearly portrayed as crucified. I would like to learn just one thing from you: Did you receive the Spirit by works of the law, or by believing what you heard? Are you so foolish? After beginning by means of the Spirit, are you now trying to finish by means of the flesh?" (3:1-3, NIV).

To turn back from *Christ-reliance* to *self-effort* is the same as to "rely on works of the law" (v. 10, RSV), and that turning means to revert to the bondage of fear (see Rom. 8:15).

Unfortunately, those who take seriously God's call to holiness often fall into the trap of slavish fear. John Wesley saw clearly that pardoning love is at the root of it all. The root of holiness is the assurance that in Christ Jesus "there is now no condemnation" (Rom. 8:1, NIV). Thank God, we are "accepted in the beloved" (Eph. 1:6). *But we must "accept our acceptance!"* In his sermon on "Satan's Devices," Wesley warns that one of Satan's most potent weapons is to cause us to doubt our acceptance by God because of our shortcomings. To give way to doubt is to forfeit first our joy, then our peace, and finally our faith and love.

We must rest in the promises of God: "There is therefore now no condemnation" if we "walk not after the flesh, but after the Spirit" (Rom. 8:1). To come to the point where we can exercise faith for the deeper blessing of heart holiness, we must maintain a joyous sense of our acceptance. We enter the experience of entire sanctification by faith alone. We begin in the Spirit, and we are perfected in the Spirit. Salvation is "by faith from first to last, just as it is written: 'The righteous will live by faith'" (Rom. 1:17, NIV).

What is the faith by which we are truly sanctified and perfected in God's love? Here is John Wesley's answer, based on Hebrews 11:1 and Romans 10:17:

> It is a divine evidence and conviction, First, that God hath promised it in the Holy Scripture. . . . It is a divine evidence and conviction, Secondly, that what God hath promised he is able to perform. . . . It is, thirdly, a divine evidence and conviction that he is able and willing to do it now. . . . To this confidence, that God is both able and willing to sanctify us now, there needs to be added one thing more—a divine evidence and conviction that he doeth it. In that hour it is done: God says to the inmost soul, "According to thy faith be it unto thee!"[1]

St. Paul prayerfully concludes, "May God himself, the God of peace, sanctify you through and through. May your whole spirit, soul and body be

THE SECRET OF HOLY LIVING

kept blameless at the coming of our Lord Jesus Christ. The one who calls you is faithful, and he will do it" (1 Thess. 5:23-24, NIV).

A Grace to Be Lived

Remember, "Christ Jesus . . . has become for us . . . holiness" (1 Cor. 1:30, NIV). To be truly sanctified is to be able to say with Paul, "My present life is not that of the old 'I,' but the living Christ within me" (Gal. 2:20, Phillips). It is to have experienced the answer to Paul's prayer in Ephesians: "that out of his glorious riches he may strengthen you with power through his Spirit in your inner being, so that Christ may dwell in your hearts through faith . . . that you may be filled to the measure of all the fullness of God" (3:16-17, 19, NIV).

To be Christian, said theologian Dietrich Bonhoeffer, is "to have the precise space once occupied by the old man now to be occupied by Jesus Christ."[2] This succinctly describes what it means to be holy, for to be truly Christian is the same thing as to be holy. Christ living and reigning in me through the power of the indwelling Spirit is the essence of holiness. The victory that overcomes the world is the faith that "greater is he that is in you, than he that is in the world" (1 John 4:4).

"If we live by the Spirit," Paul urges, "let us also walk by the Spirit" (Gal. 5:25, RSV). Walking by the Spirit is remembering that apart from Christ we "can do nothing" (John 15:5). It is maintaining a moment-by-moment dependency upon him as our Life.

At its deepest, holiness is not a matter of holy habit patterns; these are simply a cut-flower arrangement if we do not sustain an intimate relationship with Christ. But if we abide in him, his life becomes our life, his love our love, and his joy our joy.

I remember hearing the late Dr. Jack Ford of England tell of a conversation he had with a man who protested that "no one can live a holy life in this sinful world."

Ford responded, "Do you believe that Jesus Christ lived a holy life?"

"Of course," the man said. "This the Bible clearly teaches."

"The question, then, is this," Ford continued: "Will you permit *Christ* to live his holy life in *you*?"

Permitting Christ to live his life in me is the secret of holy living.

NOTES

I: Nazarene Theology in Perspective

1. *The Works of John Wesley*, 3rd ed., 14 vols. (London: Wesleyan Methodist Book Room, 1873; repr., Kansas City: Nazarene Publishing House, 1978), 5:3. Hereinafter referred to as *Works*.

2. A. M. Hills, *Fundamental Christian Theology*, 2 vols. (Pasadena, CA: C. J. Kinne, 1931), 1:134.

3. Karl Barth, *God in Action* (Manhasset, NY: Round Table Press, 1963), 47.

4. *The Writings of Arminius*, trans. James Nichols, 3 vols. (Grand Rapids: Baker Books, 1956), 1:253.

5. *The Sermons of John Wesley*, Sermon 128, "Free Grace."

6. *The Epistle to the Romans*, trans. Edwyn Hoskins (London: Oxford University Press, 1933), 314.

7. See Jürgen Moltmann, *The Theology of Hope*, trans. James W. Leitch (New York: Harper & Row, 1967).

II. John Wesley's Theology of Christian Perfection

1. George Croft Cell, *The Rediscovery of John Wesley* (New York: Henry Holt & Co., 1935), 347.

2. Ibid., 348.

3. Ibid., 359. [Recent scholarship has demonstrated that this neglect was due less to Luther himself than to subsequent Lutheran scholars.—HRD]

4. John Wesley, *The Letters of John Wesley*, ed. John Telford, 8 vols. (London: Epworth Press, 1931), 8:238.

5. Nolan B. Harmon, *Understanding the Methodist Church* (Nashville: Methodist Publishing House, 1961).

6. Colin W. Williams, *John Wesley's Theology Today* (Nashville: Abingdon Press, 1960), 167-68n.

7. Wesley, *Works*, 11:416.

8. Ibid., 394.

9. *The Standard Sermons of John Wesley*, ed. Edward H. Sugden, 2 vols. (London: Epworth Press), 2:448, 457.

10. Harald Lindstrom, *Wesley and Sanctification* (Stockholm: Nya Bokforlags Aktiebo-laget, 1946), 172.

11. *Theological Dictionary of the Bible*, ed. Gerhard Friedrich and trans. Geoffrey W. Bromiley (Grand Rapids: Eerdmans), 8:73-77.

12. Ibid., 67-68.

13. Antonio Royo, O.P., and Jordan Aumann, O.P., *The Theology of Christian Perfection* (Dubuque, IA: Priory Press, 1962), 122.

14. Ibid., 25. Royo and Aumann quote in this regard to Isa. 42:8; 48:11-12; Rev. 1:8; and 1 Cor. 10:31.

15. As quoted in Royo and Aumann, *Christian Perfection*, 25.

16. John Wesley, *Explanatory Notes upon the New Testament* (London: Epworth Press, 1950), 617. Hereinafter referred to as *Notes*.

17. Royo and Aumann, *Christian Perfection*, 26.

18. Wesley, *Notes*, 735.

19. Ibid., 910.

20. Wesley, *Works*, 11:416.

21. Ibid.

22. Ibid.

23. Ibid., 11:430.

24. Ibid., 9:456.

25. Ibid., 6:512.

26. Wesley, *Standard Sermons*, 2:446.

27. Ibid., 446-47; cf. 454. In his sermon "On Sin in Believers" Wesley demonstrates that this doctrine is not only the official position of the Church of England as expressed in the Ninth Article but also the teaching of "The Reformed Church in Europe" (except for Count Nikolaus Von Zinzendorf) and the unanimous verdict of Holy Scripture, confirmed by experience (*Standard Sermons*, 2:361-78).

28. "The Repentance of Believers," *Standard Sermons*, 2:385. "But can Christ be in the same heart where sin is? Undoubtedly He can; otherwise it could not be saved therefrom. Where the sickness is, there is the Physician.

Carrying on His work within,

Striving till He cast out sin.

Christ indeed cannot *reign* where sin *reigns*; neither will He *dwell* where sin is *allowed*. But He *is* and *dwells* in the heart of every believer, who is *fighting against* all sin; although he is not yet purified, according to the purification of the sanctuary" ("On Sin in Believers," *Standard Sermons*, 2:369).

29. Wesley, "The Scripture Way of Salvation," *Standard Sermons*, 2:447-48.

30. Cited by Williams, *John Wesley's Theology Today*, 190.

31. Ibid.

32. Wesley, *Works*, 7:486.

33. Wesley, *Letters*, 5:223.

34. Wesley, *Works*, 11:375; cf. "Christian Perfection," *Standard Sermons*, 2:162-63.

35. John N. Oswalt, "Old Testament Concept of the Holy Spirit," *Religion in Life* 48, no. 3 (Autumn 1979): 283-92.

36. John Wesley, *Explanatory Notes upon the Old Testament* (Salem, OH: Schmull Publishers, 1975), 3:2385.

37. Paul Bassett, "Conservative Wesleyan Theology and the Challenge of Secular Humanism," *Wesleyan Theological Journal* 8 (Spring 1973): 74.

38. Wesley, *Works*, 11:416.

39. Ibid., sermon "On Perfection," 6:488 (italics Wesley's).

40. Lindstrom, *Wesley and Sanctification*, 173. "Faith then was originally designed of God to establish the law of love. . . . It is the grand means of restoring that holy love wherein man was originally created. It follows that although faith is of no value in itself, (as neither is any other means whatsoever) yet as it leads to that end, the establishing anew the law of love in our hearts; and as . . . it is the only means of effecting it, it is . . . of unspeakable value to God" (Wesley, *Works*, 5:464).

41. Mildred Bangs Wynkoop, *A Theology of Love* (Kansas City: Beacon Hill Press of Kansas City, 1972), 269.

42. Lindstrom, *Wesley and Sanctification*, 141.

43. Wesley, "On Patience," *Works*, 6:488 (italics Wesley's).

44. John Wesley, *The Works of John Wesley*, ed. Albert Outler (Nashville: Abingdon Press, 1987), 4:121.

45. Ibid., "The One Thing Needful," 4:355.

46. Wesley, *Letters*, 6:68.

47. Ibid., 4:208.

48. Wesley, *Works*, 12:257.

49. Wesley, *Letters*, 6:25-26. To Charles he wrote in an even stronger vein:

One word more, concerning setting perfection too high. That *perfection* which I believe, I can boldly preach, because I think I see five hundred instances of it. Of that *perfection* which you preach, you do not think you see any witnesses at all. Why, then you must have more courage than I, or you could not persist in preaching it. I wonder you do not in this article fall in plumb with Mr. Whitefield. For do you not as well as he ask, "Where are the perfect ones?" I verily believe there are none upon earth, none dwelling in the body. I cordially assent to his opinion that *there is no such perfection* here as you describe—at least I never met with an instance of it; and I doubt I never shall. Therefore I still think that to set perfection so high is effectually to destroy it. (*Letters*, 5:20)

50. Wesley, *Works*, 11:396.

51. Ibid., 11:417. See Wesley, *Letters*, 4:189-90.

52. Williams, *John Wesley's Theology Today*, 179. "None feel their need of Christ like these; none so entirely depend upon him. For Christ does not give life to the soul separate from, but in and with, himself. . . . For our perfection is not like that of a tree, which flourishes from the sap derived from its own root, but . . . like that of a branch, united to the vine; but, severed from it, is dried up and withered" (Wesley, *Works*, 11:395-96).

53. Wesley, *Letters*, 5:322.

54. C. Ryder Smith, *The Bible Doctrine of Sin* (London: Epworth Press, 1953), 143.

55. Williams, *John Wesley's Theology Today*, 189.

56. P. T. Forsyth, *Christian Perfection* (London: Hodder & Stoughton, n.d.), 111.

57. Karl Barth, *The Epistle to the Romans*, trans. Edwyn Hoskins (London: Oxford University Press, 1933), 314.

III. On Entire Sanctification

1. These references show that Greathouse was reading widely beyond the rather limited scope of holiness resources. At this period, many holiness teachers were merely demonizing people like Reinhold Niebuhr rather than seeking to come to terms with their work. In paying attention to the wider theological world, Greathouse was a pioneer who paved the way for later Nazarene scholars. This open-minded response made him the subject of criticism by some of his closed-minded colleagues. [HRD]

2. The reference here is to W. E. Sangster, *The Path to Perfection* (New York: Abingdon-Cokesbury Press, 1943), and Reinhold Niebuhr, *The Nature and Destiny of Man* (2 vols.; London: Nisbet & Co. Ltd., 1946). These were among the earliest critiques of the holiness claim for the eradication of sin from the human heart based on the "discovery of the intractable nature of sin" as described in Mark R. Quanstrom, *A Century of Holiness Theology* (Kansas City: Beacon Hill Press of Kansas City, 2004).

3. It is fascinating how prophetic these proposals were at the time. All of them have become stress points in the ongoing attempt of the church to remain true to its commitment to the doctrine and experience of sanctification. Dr. Greathouse himself continued to wrestle with them, as is reflected in several of the essays included in this anthology. [HRD]

4. Sangster, *Path to Perfection*, 52-53.

5. Quoted by John L. Peters, *Christian Perfection and American Methodism* (New York: Abingdon Press, 1956), 39.

6. Ibid., 40.

7. W. K. Anderson, ed., *Methodism* (Cincinnati: Methodist Publishing House, 1947), 124-25.

8. F. F. Bruce, *Commentary on the Book of Acts* (Grand Rapids: Eerdmans, 1954), 35.

9. George Hendry, *The Holy Spirit in Christian Theology* (Philadelphia: Westminster Press, 1965).

IV. Who Is the Holy Spirit?

1. Cell, *Rediscovery of John Wesley*, 353.

2. Ibid.

3. John Wesley, *A Plain Account of Christian Perfection* (repr., Kansas City: Beacon Hill Press of Kansas City), 98-99.

V. The Baptism with the Holy Spirit

1. Wesley, *Notes*, 393 (on Acts 1:5).

2. Wesley, sermon "On Grieving the Holy Spirit," *Works*, 7:486.

3. Wesley, *Works*, 5:9 (italics Wesley's). This definition also sheds light on Wesley's observations on John the Baptist and Cornelius. Commenting on Jesus' claim that "he that is least in the kingdom of heaven is greater than" John, Wesley says it may mean, "The least true Christian believer has a more perfect knowledge of Jesus Christ, of His redemption and kingdom, than John the Baptist did, who died before the full manifestation of the gos-

pel" (*Notes*, 59). Of Cornelius Wesley says: "*Is accepted of him*—Through Christ, though he knows Him not. The assertion is express, and admits of no exception. He is in the favour of God, whether enjoying His written word and ordinances or not" (*Notes*, 435). And "yet it is certain, *in the Christian sense*, Cornelius was then an unbeliever" (*Notes*, 432, emphasis added).

4. Wesley, *Notes*, 368.

5. Ibid., 366, emphasis added.

6. John A. Knight, "John Fletcher's Influence on the Development of Wesleyan Theology in America," *Wesleyan Theological Journal* 13 (Spring 1978): 27-28.

7. Allan Coppedge, "Entire Sanctification in Early American Methodism, 1812-1836," *Wesleyan Theological Journal* 13 (Spring 1978): 45-46.

8. Timothy L. Smith, "The Doctrine of the Holy Spirit: Charles G. Finney's Synthesis of Wesleyan and Covenant Theology," *Wesleyan Theological Journal* 13 (Spring 1978): 117.

9. Ibid., 106.

10. Donald W. Dayton, "The Doctrine of the Baptism of the Holy Spirit: Charles G. Finney's Synthesis of Wesleyan and Covenant Theology," *Wesleyan Theological Journal* 13 (Spring 1978): 100-103.

11. Herbert McGonigle, "Pneumatological Nomenclature in Early Methodism," *Wesleyan Theological Journal* 8 (Spring 1973): 61-72.

12. See Frederick Dale Bruner, *Theology of the Holy Spirit* (Grand Rapids: Eerdmans, 1970), 323-41.

13. H. Orton Wiley, *Christian Theology*, 2 vols. (Kansas City: Nazarene Publishing House, 1947), 2:329-30.

14. Creed of Constantinople.

15. Wesley, *Notes*, 365.

16. "I believe . . . in the Holy Spirit, the holy catholic Church, the communion of saints" (Apostles' Creed).

17. John Calvin, "Minor Prophets," *Calvin's Commentaries*, 5:572.

18. See Willard H. Taylor, "The Baptism of the Holy Spirit: Promise of Grace or Judgment?" *Wesleyan Theological Journal* 12 (Spring 1977): 22. This entire article is a learned, well-documented survey of the topic of Spirit baptism with reference to Matt. 3:11-12. Even George Buttrick says of Christ's "most searching" baptism: "The ancient refiner watched the silver in the crucible, and kept the flame burning until the base metal had all come to the top and been skimmed off, until all agitation had ceased, and until he could see his face in the mirror. This is a parable of the refining fire of baptism into Christ" (*Interpreter's Bible*, 7:266).

19. For passages that speak of the divine holiness as consuming fire, see Isa. 1:25 ("I will turn my hand against you and will smelt away your dross as with lye and remove all your alloy" [RSV]) and Isa. 33:11-12, 14-15 (". . . 'your breath is a fire that will consume you. And the peoples will be as if burned to lime, like thorns cut down, that are burned in the fire.' . . . 'Who among us can dwell with the devouring fire? Who among us can dwell with the everlasting burnings?' He who walks righteously and speaks with the everlasting burnings?' He who walks righteously and speaks uprightly, who despises the gain of oppressions" [RSV]).

20. H. V. Miller, *When He Is Come* (Kansas City: Nazarene Publishing House, 1941), 10.

21. "There is a threefold reception of the Spirit," Richard S. Taylor points out—"(1) He is 'received' incognito and non-volitionally in awakening and conviction; (2) He is received as the unidentified Agent of our new birth, when we consciously receive Christ as Savior; (3) He is received consciously and volitionally as a Person in His own right, by the regenerate child of God, to indwell and rule completely as Christ's Other Self" (Myron F. Boyd and Merne A. Harris, eds., "The New Birth," *Projecting Our Heritage* [Kansas City: Beacon Hill Press of Kansas City, 1969], 61n.).

22. See John Wick Bowman, *The Intention of Jesus* (Philadelphia: Westminster Press, 1943).

23. See W. T. Purkiser, et al., *God, Man, and Salvation* (Kansas City: Beacon Hill Press of Kansas City, 1977), 494 n. 21.

VI. Sanctification and the Christus Victor Motif in Wesleyan Theology

1. Gustaf Aulen, *Christus Victor*, trans. A. G. Hebert (New York: Macmillan Co., 1951).

2. Ibid., 1-4.

3. Ibid., 5.

4. Ibid., 20-21, 41-44.

5. Ibid., 22, 31-32, 44.

6. Ibid., 22.

7. Ibid., 61-80.

8. Ibid., 6-7.

9. It was Origen (AD 185-254) who converted the *Christus Victor* idea into a theory of a ransom paid to Satan.

10. Aulen, *Christus Victor*, 71-73.

11. Ibid., n. on p. 148; cf. pp. 22-25.

12. Ibid., 50.

13. James S. Stewart, *A Faith to Proclaim* (New York: Harper & Brothers, 1957), 94.

14. C. K. Barrett, *The Epistle to the Romans* (New York: Charles Scribner's Sons, 1953), 125.

15. William Sanday and Arthur C. Headlam, *The Epistle to the Romans* (New York: Harper & Brothers, 1929), 158.

16. The key term for sin in Romans 5:12—8:10, literally "the sin" principle, which occurs at least twenty-eight times.

17. As "body" (*soma*) is my total self concretely expressed, so "flesh" (*sarx*) is my whole person alienated from God and therefore subjected to my own creaturehood and sin.

18. Karl Barth, *A Shorter Commentary on Romans* (Richmond, VA: John Knox Press, 1959), 69.

19. C. Anderson Scott, "Romans," *The Abingdon Bible Commentary* (New York: Abingdon Press, 1929), 1153.

20. C. H. Dodd, *The Epistle to the Romans* in *The Moffatt New Testament Commentary* (New York: Harper & Brothers, 1932), 93.

As Origen noted, we human beings have "the flesh of sin," but the Son had the "likeness of sinful flesh." He came in a form like us in that he became a member of the sin-oriented human race; he experienced the effects of sin and suffered death, the result of sin, as one "cursed" by the law (Gal. 3:12). Thus in his own person he coped with the power of sin. Paul's use of the phrase *sarx hamartias* denoted not the guilty human condition, but the proneness of humanity made of flesh that is oriented to sin. (Joseph Fitzmyer, "Romans" in *Anchor Bible*, 33:485)

Those who believe that it was fallen human nature which was assumed have even more cause than had the authors of the Heidelberg Catechism to see the whole of Christ's life on earth as having redemptive significance; for, in this view [which was espoused by the early church fathers], Christ's life before His actual ministry and death was not just a standing where unfallen Adam had stood without yielding to the temptation to which Adam succumbed, but a matter of starting from where we start, subjected to all the evil pressures which we inherit and using the altogether unpromising and unsuitable material of our corrupt nature to work out a perfect sinless obedience. (C. E. B. Cranfield, *Romans*, 1:383 n. 2)

Colin Gunton concurs: "To bear fallen flesh is necessary if Jesus is to complete the work to which he was called. What is important soteriologically was that Jesus was enabled to resist temptation, not by some immanent conditioning, but by virtue of his obedience to the guidance of the Spirit" (*Christ and Creation* [Grand Rapids: Eerdmans Publishing Co., 1992], 54). For *us*, gaining mastery over fallen flesh requires that we be born again, Jesus needed no second birth—his conception and birth by the Spirit enabled him to live without sinning. "[God] with the view to the destruction of sin," Gregory of Nyssa wrote, "was blended with human nature, like a sun as it were making his dwelling in a murky cave and by His presence dissipating the darkness by means of His light. For though He took our filth upon Himself, yet He is not Himself defiled by the pollution, but in His own self He purifies the filth" (*Antirrhetic adv. Apolinaris*, 26). Jesus' assumption of our fallen flesh was the *sine qua non* of our redemption, for "He could heal only what he assumed" (Gregory of Nazianzus). *He became what we are that we might become what he is.* Such was the dominating theme of the Christology of the orthodox fathers who fashioned the ecumenical creeds.

21. The first Adam disobeyed God and died; the last Adam died rather than disobey him, becoming "obedient unto death, even death on a cross. Therefore God has highly exalted him" (Phil. 2:8-9, RSV). And "being . . . exalted at the right hand of the God, and having received from the Father the promise of the Holy Spirit," he has poured out the Spirit upon yielded believers, *reproducing in us the very holiness of Christ!* (Acts 2:33, RSV). Thus the glorified Christ, through the gift of the Pentecostal Spirit, fulfills the new covenant promise of entire sanctification (Jer. 31:31-34; Ezek. 36:24-27).

22. F. Godet, *St. Paul's Epistle to the Romans* (New York: Funk and Wagnalls, 1883), 244.

23. Wesley, *Plain Account*, 62.

24. John Deschner, *Wesley's Christology* (Dallas: Southern Methodist University Press, 1960), 116.

25. He speaks of the devil as "the first sinner of the universe" (*Notes*, 1 John 3:18), who "transfused" his own self-will and pride into our first parents (Sermon CXXIII, I. 1; Sermon LXXII, I. 9-10), thus becoming the "origin of evil" in the world (*Notes*, Matt. 13:28; John 8:44; Sermon LXXII, I. 8). By sin and death Satan gained possession of the world, so that it was "Satan's house" (*Notes*, Matt. 12:29; John 12:31). Man's guilt gave him over to Satan's power, and man's corruption takes Satan's side in temptation. Satan thus enjoyed a right, a claim, and a power over man (*Notes*, John 13:39; Rom. 6:14). Christ's ministry was an assault upon Satan (*Notes*, Matt. 12:29), but his decisive encounter with Satan, sin, and death was in the cross and resurrection (*Notes*, Matt. 27:52-53; Luke 12:50; 1 Cor. 15:26; Eph. 4:8; Heb. 2:14). The resurrection, which is victory over death, is the inauguration of Christ's kingdom (*Notes*, Luke 22:16; Acts 2:31; 1 Cor. 15:26), and its power will raise men to new life in regeneration and eternal life in the general resurrection (*Notes*, Rom. 6:5; Eph. 1:19; 1 Cor. 15:20). The ascension signifies Christ's exaltation to the Father's right hand (Acts 2:33; Eph. 1:21-22) until he returns to judge the world (*Notes*, Rev. 1:7; Heb. 9:28). After the judgment Christ will return the mediatorial kingdom to the Father but will continue to reign eternally with him (*Notes*, 1 Cor. 15:24). Here, indeed, are the essential elements of a full *Christus Victor* doctrine. See Deschner, *Wesley's Christology*, chap. 5, "The Kingly Work of Christ," and William M. Greathouse, "John Wesley's View of the Last Things," *The Second Coming: A Wesleyan Approach to the Doctrine of the Last Things* (Kansas City: Beacon Hill Press of Kansas City, 1995), 142-48.

26. Williams, *John Wesley's Theology Today*, 88.

27. Scripture references hereafter are all to Wesley's *Explanatory Notes upon the New Testament*.

28. Wesley, Sermon LXXII, "The End of Christ's Coming" (II. 7; III. 1, 1).

29. Deschner, *Wesley's Christology*, 105.

30. Randy L. Maddox, "Reconnecting the Means to the End: A Wesleyan Prescription for the Holiness Movement," *Wesleyan Theological Journal* 33 (Fall 1988): 29-66; Henry H. Knight III, *The Presence of God in the Christian Life: John Wesley and the Means of Grace* (Metuchen, NJ & London: Scarecrow Press, 1992).

31. Wesley, Sermon XXI, Discourse I, "Upon our Lord's Sermon on the Mount" (I. 11).

32. Wesley, *Plain Account*, 81, 83.

33. Ibid., 62.

34. Wesley, sermon "The Means of Grace," *Standard Sermons*, 1:238. By the instituted means of grace Wesley understood (1) Prayer, (2) Searching the Scriptures, (3) Fasting, (4) Christian Conference (Colin Williams, *John Wesley's Theology Today*, 132-36). The private means of grace he subdivided as (1) works of piety and (2) works of mercy (Theodore Runyon, *The New Creation: John Wesley's Theology Today* [Nashville: Abingdon Press, 1998], 106-7).

VII. Sin: A Wesleyan Definition

1. Wesley, *Plain Account*, 23.

2. See Wesley, *Works*, 12:239.

3. Wesley, sermon "Justification by Faith," in *Works*, 5:57.

4. Wesley, *Notes*, Rom. 4:5: "Christ here interposes; justice is satisfied; the sin is remitted, and pardon is applied to the soul by a divine faith wrought by the Holy Ghost, who then begins the great work of inward sanctification. Thus God justifies the ungodly, and yet remains just, and true to all his attributes" (532).

5. Wesley, *Letters*, 5:322 (italics added).

6. *Luther's Works*, Weimar Edition, 54:180.

7. Wesley, *Notes*, 911.

8. Wesley, *Plain Account*, 54.

9. Ibid., 81, 83.

10. Ibid.

11. This text, a summary of Rom. 5:12—8:39, was the core of Wesley's gospel; his Journals record that he "offered Christ" from it more than seventy-two times during his lifetime.

VIII. The Dynamics of Sanctification: Biblical Terminology

1. Georgia Harkness, *The Fellowship of the Holy Spirit* (Nashville: Abingdon Press, 1966), 92.

2. "Let this perfection appear in its native form, and who can speak one word against it?" Wesley asks. "It must be disguised before it can be opposed" (*Plain Account*, 118).

3. This refers to the methodology stemming from the teaching of Mrs. Phoebe Palmer, whose influence on the nineteenth-century holiness movement was extensive. She taught that the acquisition of entire sanctification was the automatic consequence of putting one's all on the altar. Since "the altar sanctifies the gift," one is immediately sanctified. [HRD]

4. A thoughtful reading of Wesley's *Plain Account of Christian Perfection* will quickly reveal how seriously this "folk theology" has departed from the more scriptural Wesleyan view of sanctification.

5. William Hordern, *New Directions in Theology Today*, Vol. 1, Introduction (Philadelphia: Westminster Press, 1966), 96-113.

6. Ibid., 99. See Karl Barth, *Church Dogmatics* (Naperville, IL: Alec. R. Allenson, 1958), IV/2; Hordern's *New Directions* (103-9) gives a summary of Barth's view of sanctification. Barth says: "What is forgiveness of sins (however we understand it) if it is not directly accompanied by an actual liberation from the committal of sin? . . . What is faith without obedience?" (*Church Dogmatics*, IV/2, 508). See also Karl Barth, *A Shorter Commentary on Romans*, esp. on chs. 6—8. On Rom. 6:6 he comments:

This is our knowledge of Jesus Christ on which our faith is founded—that the "old man," i.e., we ourselves, as God's enemies, have been crucified and killed in and with the crucifixion of the man Jesus at Golgotha, so that the "body" (i.e., the subject, the person needed for the doing) of sin, the man who can sin and will sin and shall sin has been removed, destroyed, done away with, is simply no longer there (and has therefore not merely been "made powerless"). (69)

7. See Hordern's bibliography on chap. 4. An exciting Roman Catholic treatment of Rom. 6—8 is found in Hans Küng, *The Church* (New York: Sheed and Ward, 1967), 150-62. Under the general topic of "The Church as the Creation of the Spirit" (150-203) Küng

develops a theology of sanctification as the work of the Holy Spirit, holding closely to biblical exposition throughout.

8. Robert E. Chiles, *Theological Transition in American Methodism: 1790-1936* (Nashville: Abingdon Press, 1966).

9. *Manual of the Church of the Nazarene*, Art. 7. [This article has since been retitled more appropriately as "Prevenient Grace."—HRD]

10. "The entire depravation of the whole human nature, of every man born into the world, in every faculty of his soul, not so much by those particular vices which reign in particular persons, as by the floods of atheism and idolatry, of pride, self-will, and love of the world is the grand distinguishing point between Heathenism and Christianity. Here is the shibboleth. Is man by nature filled with all manner of evil? Is he void of all good? Is he wholly fallen? Is his soul totally corrupted? Allow this, and you are so far a Christian. Deny it and you are but a heathen still" (Wesley, cited by Cell, *Rediscovery of John Wesley*, 278).

11. "To grace I ascribe the commencement, the continuation, and the consummation of all good" (Arminius, *Works*, 1:253). At this point Wesleyan Arminianism stands "within a hair's breadth of Calvinism."

12. "The new concern with sanctification," Hordern reminds us,

has not arisen from a more optimistic view of human capacities than was held by the earlier neoorthodox theology. The doctrine of sanctification is seen in closest relationship to the doctrine of justification. Man, in his sin, cannot save himself, and even the justified sinner cannot make himself righteous by his own efforts. Whereas many liberals accepted only a moral influence theory of the atonement, the new concern with sanctification almost always presupposed that an objective difference was made in man's relationship to God because Christ bore the price of sin and rose from the dead to defeat the powers of evil. There is a real optimism in this concern for sanctification, but it is an optimism about the grace of God, not about the ability of man. (*New Directions*, 101)

13. This holiness communicates itself to the surrendered worshiper (Isa. 6:5; cf. 33:14), but the unyielding will be consumed along with his sin (Heb. 12:29; Mal. 4:1). Since God is absolute holiness Jesus said, "Every one will be salted with fire" (Mark 9:49, RSV; see vv. 43-50), either the fire of Pentecost or the fire of Gehenna.

14. Turning his freedom *in* God to freedom *from* God (Gen. 3:1-6; Isa. 14:12-14; Ezek. 28:2), sin is essentially self-sovereignty, self-rule, inordinate self-love, self-idolatry. Bertrand Russell once said, "Every man would like to be God if it were possible; some few refuse to admit the impossibility." In his essay on the meaning of existentialism, Jean-Paul Sartre affirms that it is "the project of man to become God."

15. Both forms of original sin are explicated in Romans. In 1:18-25 it is pictured as the prideful refusal of the creature "to glorify God as God," the refusal of man to recognize his creaturehood and feel his grateful dependence upon God, his stubborn unwillingness to serve and worship his Creator. He worships and serves the creature rather than the Creator. Consequently, man is subjected to the creature and tyrannized by the flesh. The frightening catalogue of sins that follows (1:25-31) is the fruit of man's sinful pride and idolatry. In 7:7-25 original sin is seen as the attempt of the religious man to find goodness and wholeness by his own moral endeavor ("by the law" of Moses or any system of morals). The would-be law-keeper finds himself weak and powerless in the face of this endeavor to

achieve holiness by the flesh; he discovers thereby the exceeding sinfulness of sin, indwelling sin, which disintegrates his personality. He discovers himself sinking in moral quicksand, in desperate need of Another who from above can lift him out of the flesh into the Spirit. That Other is Jesus Christ. In his attempt to achieve righteousness and wholeness by the law, sinful man succeeds only into turning that law, which is essentially "spiritual," into "the law of sin and death." Original sin is thus a dynamic reality. It is no "thing like substance," as Sugden thought Wesley believed and as others have charged; it is rather a false condition of egocentricity (with all the attendant sins generated by the "flesh," or the creature cut off from God), a consequence of man's broken relationship with his Creator—not a biological but a theological fact. Since man is alienated from the life of God, he is corrupt through deceitful lusts (see Eph. 4:17-19).

16. "All things are of God, who hath reconciled us to himself by Jesus Christ" (2 Cor. 5:18; see vv. 18-21).

17. "But of him [God] are ye in Christ Jesus, who of God is made unto us wisdom, and righteousness, and sanctification, and redemption: that, according as it is written, He that glorieth, let him glory in the Lord" (1 Cor. 1:30-31).

18. Cf. Deut. 7:6. As God separated ancient Israel to himself by the redemption he wrought at the Red Sea (Exod. 20:1 ff.; cf. 1 Kings 8:51, 53), he separated the new "Israel of God" (Gal. 6:16) to himself by "the Exodus which he [Christ] accomplished at Jerusalem" (Luke 9:31, literal translation) (1 Pet. 1, 18-21; 1 Cor. 6:19-20).

19. In the law, the cultic and the ethical seem to be intermingled with no effort to distinguish the one from the other (see Lev. 19 for the most obvious illustration of this fact).

20. Isaiah 5:16 is indicative of this fact. It reads: "But the LORD of hosts is exalted in justice, and the Holy God shows himself holy ["sanctified" (KJV)] in righteousness" (RSV).

21. The reason Christ did not use these words was because these terms had only a cultic meaning in the Judaism of that time. See Matt. 23:16-28, where Jesus contrasts his prophetic demand for "justice and mercy and faith" (v. 23, RSV) with the pharisaical for ceremonial purity. Here Jesus sounds much like Amos (Amos 5:21-27), Hosea (Hos. 6:6; cf. Matt. 9:13), and Micah (Mic. 6:8). Yet see Matt. 6:9, "Our Father who art in heaven, sanctified be thy name." For Jesus holiness meant wholeness of devotion to God (Matt. 6:9-10; Mark 12:28-30), the integrity of perfect love (Matt. 5:17—6:34).

22. Rom. 8:9: "You are not in the flesh, you are in the Spirit, if the Spirit of God really dwells in you" (cf. Rom. 7:17, 20, where to be "in the flesh" means to be controlled by "sin which dwells within me" [RSV]).

23. Aulen, *Christus Victor.* See essay on this subject in this collection.

24. Rom. 6:1-14, esp. v. 6. Hordern says:

Harrisville argues that the New Testament never treats the new birth in terms of the believer as an isolated entity. Paul always sees man's life in a "field of being." He is "in Adam" or he is "in Christ." For Paul these are not abstractions; they are empirical realities. To be "in Adam" is to be identified with the society of unbelieving mankind. It is to express the spirit of one's age and social environment. To be "in Christ" is not a matter of an individualistic psychological experience of salvation; it is to be identified with the

119

community that confesses Christ as Lord. Apart from the community of those who are the body of Christ, the church, there is no new birth, no sanctification. (*New Directions*, 110)

25. "To be 'in Christ' is to be incorporated in the newly created humanity, the new supernatural community or order of relationships, the new 'body,' which has come into existence through and around Christ. The essential fact about the believer is that he is no longer 'in Adam'; he is 'in Christ.' He is no longer a 'natural man'; he is a 'spiritual man'" (John Knox, "Romans," in *The Interpreter's Bible*, 12 vols. [Nashville: Abingdon Press, 1951], 9:473).

26. Here the words translated "sin" are *he hamartia* ("the sin"). *He hamartia* is the principle of revolt issuing in many transgressions, the sin principle; the phrase occurs twenty-eight times between Rom. 5:12 and 8:10.

27. Dodd, *Epistle of Paul to the Romans*, 82.

28. Küng, *The Church*, 152. Kung continues:

God himself must free the man who is unfree and incapable of winning his own freedom, must free him for freedom. He can turn "slaves of sin" into "slaves of God," who have been "set free from sin" (Rom. 6:20, 22). God does this for the man who believes, whether Jew or Gentile, through his eschatological act of salvation in Jesus Christ. In Christ, the new free man, God promised and revealed and created the way to a new and true freedom. (Ibid.)

29. "Is the Christian truly redeemed and freed?" Küng asks.

Despite the fact that the revelation and perfection of his redemption is still in the future, . . . the believing Christian can already be a redeemed person, freed from sin, law and death. This can of course only be understood in the context of faith, and certainly only lived in the context of faith. But if a man has accepted in faith the message of freedom in Christ, and if he strives to live in that faith, then he truly experiences freedom, he is a free man in the way that a Jew waiting for his salvation under the law never can be. (Ibid., 159)

30. Charles W. Lowry, *The Trinity and Christian Devotion* (New York: Harper & Brothers, 1946), 74.

31. Ibid., 73.

32. "Therefore whoever disregards this, disregards not man but God, who gives his Holy Spirit to you" (1 Thess. 4:8, RSV).

33. Cell, *Rediscovery of John Wesley*, 353. In this vein John Wesley wrote, "I believe in the infinite and eternal Spirit of God equal with the Father and the Son, to be not only holy in himself, but the immediate cause of all holiness in us; enlightening our understandings, rectifying our wills and affections, renewing our natures, uniting our persons to Christ, assuring us of the adoption of sons, leading us in our actions, purifying and sanctifying our souls and bodies, to the full enjoyment of God."

34. It is because our nineteenth-century holiness fathers were forced to preserve this truth as over against a mere gradualistic theory that they tended to speak of sanctification almost altogether in this restricted sense. In the polemic of the day, "sanctification" came to be identified almost exclusively with "the second work of grace." This process had begun earlier, however, with Adam Clarke, probably under the same general set of circumstances. Unlike Wesley and Fletcher, Clarke ruled out altogether the idea of gradual sanctification. He states, "In no part of Scripture are we directed to seek holiness grada-

tim. We are to come to God as well for an instantaneous and complete purification from all sin, as for an instantaneous pardon" (cited by Peters, *Christian Perfection and American Methodism*, 106).

35. Although Wesley did not usually identify the "baptism" with the Spirit as the moment of entire sanctification, there seems to be ample basis for seeing the baptism, the infilling, and the gift of the Spirit as experientially synonymous in Acts (see Kenneth Geiger, ed., *The Word and the Doctrine* [Kansas City: Beacon Hill Press of Kansas City, 1965], 215-23, for the use of the terms in both Acts and Wesley).

36. The reader is referred to a most illuminating critical treatment of this topic in Victor Paul Furnish, *Theology and Ethics in Paul* (Nashville: Abingdon Press, 1968), 171-81, 194-98. This exegetical study of Rom. 6:1—7:6 illustrates the point I made earlier that much current New Testament exegesis is wholly congenial to the Wesleyan understanding of holiness.

37. Because the gift of the Spirit comes through union with Christ in his death and resurrection, the New Testament sometimes speaks of Christ as "the Spirit." See 1 Cor. 15:15b; 2 Cor. 3:17-18. In Rom. 8:9, "the Spirit of God" is used interchangeably with "the Spirit of Christ." These passages are not to be interpreted in such a way as to make of Paul a binitarian, but as indicative of the fact that the work of the Spirit is indissolubly linked with Christ's redemption (see John 7:39; Acts 2:33) and as supporting the truth that it is the Spirit's work to form Christ in the believer (see John 16:13-15). See Küng, *The Church*, 166-67.

38. See 2 Cor. 5:14-15, RSV. The KJV's "then were all dead" entirely misses Paul's point.

39. The specialized form of the pronoun *hoitines* (pronoun of quality—"people such as we") gives the sense. "We cannot as Christians go on living in sin because as Christians we have died to sin. . . . The definite past tense, 'we died,' points to a particular moment; conversion and (as the next verse shows) baptism must be in mind" (C. K. Barrett, *The Epistle to the Romans* in *Harper's New Testament Commentaries* [New York: Harper & Bros., 1957], 121). See Furnish, *Theology and Ethics*, 171-73, where he says with respect to the question of Rom. 6:1:

For Paul an affirmative answer is unthinkable, for the declaration that grace "reigns" (5:21) is at the same time a declaration that sin's power has been broken. This is the meaning of the statement that the Christian has "died to sin" (6:2). *The point is that the power of sin (which is the law, I Cor. 15:56) is incompatible with the power of grace*, and further on in his argument the apostle specifically says that "sin will exercise no dominion over you [*hypon ou kyrieyse*], for you are not under [the power of the] law [*hypo nomon*] but under [the power of] grace [*hypo chariin*] (vs. 14). The event of grace, as the whole of this portion of Romans shows, is the event of Christ's death-resurrection and the believer's participation in it. . . . Since Christ's death is God's way of meeting and overcoming sin, it may be said that Christ "died to sin, once for all" (Rom. 6:10 RSV). As an act of obedience to God (5:19) and thus righteousness (5:18), Christ's death is the actualization of God's power and puts an effective check on sin's tyrannical hold. . . . The believer's death with Christ has the same result. . . . "All who belong to Christ have crucified the flesh with its passions and desires" (Gal. 5:24 RSV), and "I [have been crucified] to the world" (Gal. 6:14 RSV).

40. Says Wesley, "They who are of Christ, who abide in him, 'have crucified the flesh with its affections and lusts.' . . . Is it good, that the whole body of sin, which is now crucified in them, should be destroyed? It shall be done!" (Sermon VIII, "The First Fruits of the Spirit," *Works*, 5:88, 96).

41. As the burial of Christ put his death to sin out of the realm of subjective experience into the realm of historical fact, the believer's baptism makes his death to sin an objectively verifiable fact: only the dead are buried. "It is only the believer who is baptized, and so baptism as 'burial' presumes that the 'death' has already occurred! . . . The priority here is with what God has accomplished through Christ. Baptism as such does not constitute the 'event of grace' but is one aspect only of the whole event" (Furnish, *Theology and Ethics*, 174).

42. "Glory" (Rom. 6:4) is an eschatological term, another indication that the quickened believer has entered the eschatological kingdom of God.

43. That is, sin has lost its legal claim upon him and therefore its power of control over him. Yet, a distinction should be made. "It is not *sin* but the *sinner* who has 'died' (vss. 2, 10, 11; cf. 7:4, death to the law). To eak of being 'freed' from sin (vss. 7, 18, 22) implies that sin still seeks to enslave, even though, being 'dead' to it, one no longer stands under its dominion (vs. 14)" (Furnish, *Theology and Ethics*, 173). To say that the justified believer has "died to sin" means therefore that he has now "freedom from the power of sin" (ibid.). In Wesley's terminology, the reign of sin is broken in the new birth (*Works*, 5:149). The references are to Rom. 6.

44. See 1 Cor. 6:9-11, on which Wesley comments: "'Ye are washed,' says the apostle, 'ye are sanctified,' namely, cleansed from 'fornication, idolatry, drunkenness,' and all other outward sin; and yet, at the same time, in another sense of the word, they were unsanctified; they were not washed, not inwardly cleansed from envy, evil surmising, partiality" (Sermon XIII, "On Sin in Believers," *Works*, 5:150). In *The Plain Account*, Wesley asks: "When does inward sanctification begin?" He answers: "In the moment a man is justified. (Yet sin remains in him, yea, the seed of all sin, till he is sanctified throughout.) From that time a believer gradually dies to sin, and grows in grace" (*Works*, 11:387).

45. "Reckon" translates *logizesthe*, an accounting term. C. H. Dodd calls the point of Rom. 6:11 a "momentous conclusion" (*Epistle of Paul to the Romans*, 91). Charles Hodge observes: "If in point of fact believers are partakers of the death and life of Christ; if they die with him, and live with him, then they should so regard themselves. They should receive this truth, with all its consoling and sanctifying power, into their hearts, and manifest it in their lives" (*Commentary on the Epistle to the Romans* [repr., Grand Rapids: Eerdmans, 1950], 201). "Reckon thus," says Joseph Agar Beet, "the nails which pierced His sacred hands and feet destroyed my old self. Christ and we were separated from sin by the same mysterious death; and therefore we are dead with Christ" (*St. Paul's Epistle to the Romans* [London: Hodder & Stoughton, 1885], 181). Here the believer "enters actively into the divine thought" (Godet)—viz., that the final object God had in mind in crucifying the believer's old man (Rom. 6:6) was his complete sanctification.

46. "The believer is to put himself at God's disposal [*paristanai*, vss. 13, 16, 11]," Furnish observes, "just as completely and obediently as the slave is to put himself at the disposal of his master." There is a difference, however, since life under the power of law

is "abject capitulation" to sin; whereas life under grace is a life of freedom (Gal. 5:1, 13). The believer is now "freed from sin" (Rom. 6:7). As the Lord's freedman, he is now to put himself voluntarily under the lordship of Christ in obedience to the grace he provided by his redemption (Rom. 5:17). Furnish says, "For Paul, obedience means surrender to God's power but not abject capitulation to it; the new Lord not only asks all, but gives all" (*Theology and Ethics*, 194-95).

47. This consecration corresponds with "perfecting holiness" (2 Cor. 7:1); it is to be "sanctified wholly" (*holoteleis*, "entirely and perfectly," 1 Thess. 5:23); it is also to be "filled with the Spirit" (Eph. 5:18; cf. Eph. 3:14-20), and "blameless in love" (Eph. 1:4; cf. 1 Thess. 3:13; Eph. 5:25-27). The reader is referred to the earlier section, where the *Christus Victor* motif is shown to imply the destruction of sin. As W. E. Sangster says, this is "a big, bold thing to believe," but to deny the possibility of this expulsion of sin from the believer's heart is to stultify the whole argument of Romans 5:12-21 and thus to deny the plain statement of Scripture, that "For this purpose the Son of God was manifested, that he might destroy the works of the devil" (1 John 3:8b). This is not the destruction of sin *per se*, but more technically its "expulsion" from the heart and life of the believer: since the believer is cautioned against falling back under its power through disobedience, sin and death remain a live possibility for the believer until his period of probation is concluded (Rom. 6:15-23). See *Beacon Bible Commentary* (Kansas City: Beacon Hill Press of Kansas City, 1968), 8:145 fn.

48. NEB (*paristanete*). In v. 19 the result is said to be *hagiasmon*. Although rendered "holiness" by the KJV, in many instances where it occurs in the New Testament (Rom. 6:19, 22; 1 Cor. 1:30; 1 Thess. 4:3-4, 7; 2 Thess. 2:13; 1 Tim. 2:15; Heb. 12:14; 1 Pet. 1:2) the ARV and NASB render *hagiasmon* "sanctification"; in most instances the RSV does the same. George Allen Turner says *hagiasmon* "connotes state and that not as native to its subject but as an outcome of action or progress" (*The More Excellent Way* [Winona Lake, IN: Light and Life Press]).

49. "For he does not give them light, but from moment to moment: the instant He withdraws, all is darkness . . . for God does not give them a stock of holiness. But unless they receive a supply every moment, nothing but unholiness would remain" (Wesley, *Works*, 11:417).

50. Ibid., 5:88; John 15:1-8.52. As "the power of sin" (1 Cor. 15:56, RSV).

51. Furnish, *Theology and Ethics*, 179.

52. To be "in the flesh" (Rom. 8:8) is not necessarily a matter of sensuality; it is living apart from God, either in rebellion (Rom. 1:20-25) or in self-effort (dependence upon the arm of flesh, rather than upon God's grace in Christ proffered through the indwelling Spirit; Rom. 7:14-25). To move from Romans 7 into Romans 8, therefore, involves the end of that dependence upon one's own works. It is thus experientially synonymous with the rest of faith (see Heb. 4:1-11, esp. vv. 9-11).

53. This progressive transfiguration of the yielded believer is also set forth in Rom. 12:2.

54. The church is "invisible" in the sense that its true life is the life of the Holy Spirit, which is secretly given by God alone; the power of the church is the power of the indwelling, sanctifying Spirit of God. But the church is also "visible," for the New Testament

knows only that church which is made up of new men in Christ who have been baptized by water into its communal life. There were simply no unbaptized Christians in New Testament times except perhaps catechumens who were in process of preparation for church membership. "Nor would it have been natural for Paul or any contemporary to consider the question whether faith without baptism made one a member of Christ's Body, while the case of a person seeking baptism without faith (however rudimentary) would have seemed too abnormal to deserve notice" (Dodd, *Epistle to the Romans*, 86).

55. To "grow up into Christ" is therefore a social experience in which "we all come in the unity of the faith . . . unto a perfect man, unto the measure of the stature of the fulness of Christ" (Eph. 4:13). The entire passage with which we have been dealing (Rom. 5—8) is predicated on the assumption that Christ and Adam are "fields of being." As a man of the flesh, the unbeliever is "in Adam"—i.e., in the society of the unredeemed where sin reigns. The believer, however, is "in Christ"—i.e., in the society of the redeemed where "grace reign[s] through righteousness unto eternal life" (Rom. 5:21), or in the body of Christ conceived of as the new man "which after God is created in righteousness and true holiness" (Eph. 4:24).

56. For this reason I modified the title of this paper, which was assigned to be on the topic "The Dynamics of *Personal* Sanctification," etc. "There is no holiness but social holiness."

57. Hordern, *New Directions*, 112-13; cf. Rom. 1:11-12.

58. That is, between the first and second advents of Christ. George Eldon Ladd speaks of the overlapping of the ages; "between the times" there is an overlapping of This Present Age and The Age to Come (*The Gospel of the Kingdom* [Grand Rapids: Eerdmans, 1950], 41-42). "The present evil age" (Gal. 1:4, RSV, etc.) continues even though "the powers of the age to come" (Heb. 6:5, RSV) have already broken into history in the death and resurrection of Christ and his exaltation to the Father's right hand as the Lord of the church who gives the Spirit to his people. Furnish writes: "God's power is nevertheless already effective for men in Christ. The two ages 'meet,' as it were, in him through whom God is even in the present reconciling the world unto himself (II Cor. 5:19)" (*Theology and Ethics*, 126). For the eschatological nature of Christ's salvation, see ibid., 115-35, 214-16.

59. "The salvation which is already present is not, therefore, somehow qualitatively preliminary or second-rate. What is given is present in its fullness (although there is, still something *not* given—namely resurrection from the dead and the final cosmic triumph of God's power over death)" (Furnish, *Theology and Ethics*, 215).

60. Ibid., 313.

61. Wesley, *Works*, 11:396.

62. Ibid., 414-19; cf. Rom. 3:23b.

63. Using "flesh" therefore in the Old Testament sense of human weakness, we must confess with Paul at all times, "The life which I now live in the flesh I live by the faith of the Son of God" (Gal. 2:20).

64. The sense of *teteleiomai*.

65. Forsyth, *Christian Perfection*, 111. God's grace had pulled Paul's personality into a unity of purpose, which "willed one thing." Thus 3:13-14 defines the meaning of present perfection—i.e., heart purity.

66. Barth, *Epistle to the Romans*, 315.

Paul's eschatological thinking always combines the perfect tense of the raising of Jesus with the future tense of the eschatological future. Both are seen in a context in which each is the ground of the other. The primitive Christian confession "that Jesus died and is risen," is thus expounded in a way totally different from the mystery cult of the dying rising God. The Christ event is presented within the framework of an eschatological expectation of what is to come, and the future expectation is grounded in the Christ event. I Thess. 4.14 ("if we believe *that* Jesus *died* and *rose* again, even so them also which sleep in Jesus *will* God bring with him") is as typical of this as is the confession of I Cor. 15.3-5 in I Cor. 15.20 ff. In all this, the connection between the resurrection of Jesus and the future which is expected is . . . mutually complementary: If there is no resurrection of the dead, then neither is Christ risen. If Christ is risen, then the dead will rise and Christ "must" reign over all his enemies, including also death. It is . . . a *dei* ("must") in terms of . . . the future necessity and future tendency inherent in the event of the resurrection of Jesus. (Moltmann, *Theology of Hope*, 162 fn.)

IX. The Significance of Water Baptism

1. All Scripture quotations in this chapter are from the Revised Standard Version of the Bible.

X. My Vision for Nazarene Worship

1. James R. Spruce, *Come, Let Us Worship* (Kansas City: Beacon Hill Press of Kansas City, 1986), 9.

2. Ibid., 10.

3. E. A. Girvin, *A Prince in Israel* (Kansas City: Beacon Hill Press, 1916), 109.

4. Quoted in Spruce, *Come, Let Us Worship*, 9.

5. Ibid., 52.

6. Ibid.

7. Ibid.

8. Ibid., 54.

9. Ibid.

10. Robert E. Webber, *Worship Old and New* (Grand Rapids: Zondervan, 1982).

11. Spruce, *Come, Let Us Worship*, 74-75.

XI. Holiness: Why All the Confusion?

1. Wesley, *Letters*, 3:9.

2. Lowry, *Trinity and Christian Devotion*, 73.

3. From 1 Thess. 5:23 and Mark 12:28-34.

4. Wesley, *Works*, 6:46, 52.

5. Wesley, *Works*, 11:401.

6. Ibid., 6:509.

7. The word *wholly* found in 1 Thess. 5:23 (*holoteleis*) occurs only here. It is the combination of the ideas of wholeness and completion. Lightfoot suggests the meaning may be given here as "may he sanctify you so that you may be entire." The next verse is a prayer that those thus made whole may be preserved in blamelessness and health.

8. Wesley, *Letters*, 4:189.

9. Wesley, *Works*, 11:417.

XII. The Secret of Holy Living

1. Wesley, "The Scripture Way of Salvation," *Works*, 6:52-53.

2. See Dietrich Bonhoeffer, *Ethics*, ed. Eberhard Bethge (New York: Macmillan Co., 1965), 41.

www.ingramcontent.com/pod-product-compliance
Lightning Source LLC
LaVergne TN
LVHW021353080426
835508LV00020B/2267